IN THE STORM OF LIFE

*How to use spiritual support
to create success with ease*

VERENA MARTIN

Copyright © 2020 Verena Martin

All rights reserved.

No part of this book may be reproduced in any manner, mechanically or electronically, including tape or other audio recordings and photocopying, without the written permission of the author, except for reasonable excerpts for research and reviewing purposes.

ISBN: 978-1-77605-673-6

Published by Kwarts Publishers
www.kwartspublishers.co.za

Contact the author:
E-mail: verena@verenamartin.online
Website: verenamartin.online

This book is dedicated to the memory of
my parents, Marlies and Hans Martin.

*Their love guides and supports me
to this very day.*

VERENA MARTIN

CONTENTS

PROLOGUE   9

1	Why We Have More Potential Than We Think	11
2	The Illusion of Fear	23
3	Life Is Never Logical	35
4	Why We Need to Be Alone	43
5	The Truth About Dualism	53
6	Stop Analyzing, Start Living	65
7	At the Core…Your Emotions	75
8	Give That Which You Want for Yourself	87
9	The Importance of Self-Definition	95
10	The Illusion of Security	103
11	The Power of Thoughts	109
12	The Illusion of Your Comfort Zone	117
13	Let Your Higher Consciousness Take Over	125
14	Visualization as a Manifestation Tool	133

15	Using Affirmations and Hypnosis as Your Power Sources	141
16	How to Use Your Intuition	151
17	The Power of Gratitude: It's All About Vibration	161

PROLOGUE

As I was sitting in my apartment in Cape Town, looking at the ocean glistening in the sun, I realized that some months ago I put this exact kind of apartment on my vision board. When I placed such a beautiful home on the board, I wondered how the universe could actually make this happen for me. You see, I want to rent, but normally these types of apartments are only available for purchase. Nevertheless, I left it to the universe to see what would happen.

Right after that, life changed dramatically when the Corona Virus crisis hit not just South Africa, but the world. During the pandemic, I spent a lot of time alone and used that time to meditate and connect with what I truly desire. After much reflection, I decided that as much as I love Cape Town, I really wanted to move back to Europe, specifically the South of France. I therefore changed my vision board to reflect the new home and life I wanted there.

However, the universe hadn't forgotten my original vision. It turned out that for the remaining months I would be spending in South Africa, the universe manifested something wonderful for me. The perfect apartment, in my building and within my budget – a beautiful penthouse with a full ocean view – became available for rent. At any other time that would be impossible, but there it was, ready for me to take and enjoy. Of course, I received what the universe gave me with immense gratitude and joy.

What happened to me is yet another confirmation that when I put my spiritual principles in place, I have the power to create whatever I desire for my life. This is a great gift, and I want to share it with you. So, my dear friends, the following pages will detail for you my personal bible, which I discovered over many years of meeting many spiritual people in many different countries. It's helped me so much to gain success with ease. Please join me and learn to use your spiritual power and potential to create your own life and make wonderful things happen for you.

With love,

Verena

WHY WE HAVE MORE POTENTIAL THAN WE THINK

WHEN WE THINK OF AN ATOM, WHAT do we imagine? Something really small, I would venture to guess. We all learned in High School that everything is composed of atoms. However, here's something we weren't all taught: Even the smallest atom is not static. It's always moving because at the base of everything in existence – even a stone – is energy and energy vibrates all the time. So, every atom of every molecule of everything in existence is made from energy and even if we can't see any of it move with the naked eye, it's all vibrating.

This has some really fascinating implications when we realize that since we all belong to this universe, the same is true with us. Every atom of our being has been created from energy so we're part of and aligned with the vibration of everything that exists. It gets even more mind-blowing.

When we allow ourselves to embrace the fact that we ourselves are a part of the energy and vibration, we can then use this knowledge (which equals power) to make our own reality and achieve the success we desire.

We can create more success than we ever dreamed imaginable because energy allows us to move things with our thoughts, intentions and emotions. They make vibrations and these pulsations are like waves which either push something away or pull it in toward us. To use an analogy, I often think about what happens when we throw a pebble into a calm lake. It makes circles. That's a good way to visualize the rippling effect which energy and vibration can cause because of one action, especially when we imagine it in terms of our life's circumstances.

There is a basic truth to which we all need to adhere before we move on: We are here for a purpose. We have chosen this lifetime wisely to make particular experiences. Nothing happens without a reason. We're not victims of circumstances because we create many of them ourselves through actions, then reactions, then actions once again. And we attract everything in our lives with our thoughts, feelings, vibration and energy. That's the reason why we are the creator of our lives. We are energy and so is everything else. That's the connection between everything that exists.

Even with this knowledge, why do so many people feel like victims all of the time? Why are they consistently anxious? The problem is that our minds are extremely limited. When we use only our brains to fathom things, we can't imagine that we have the power and energy within ourselves to dictate the terms of our destiny. This leaves us feeling helpless and causes anxiety, which we'll talk about a great deal throughout this book. The fact is, our souls know so much more than our minds ever could. So, we shouldn't be so hard on ourselves. It's all part of our human existence. We were trained by our parents and society to be super realistic and to not believe in things we can't immediately see with our eyes or measure with our brains – such as energy and vibrations. That's why we aren't fully aware of what awesome things we're really capable of doing.

Keeping all of this in mind, we begin to see that it's not our mind but our soul and emotions that are our most powerful tools because they can create any vibration that we want. So, it's very important to use our energy and vibrations the right way and to be very aware that what we think is even more powerful than what we do sometimes.

We may not realize it, but we're in total control of whether or not we'll have a good or a bad day. For instance, Joanne might walk out of the house on a rainy morning and accidentally step into a messy puddle. "Ugh," she thinks! As she heads down the block, a strong gust of wind turns her umbrella inside out and it breaks. Now she's soaked and she's thinking, "This is going to be one of those days." That thought is a mistake, but maybe she'll forget about it and be more positive until, of course, her heel breaks when she steps into a crack in the curb. "That's it," she shouts! "It's going to be a miserable day!" She arrives at work in a solemn mood and her energy level decreases.

Joanne put out lots of negative vibrations that morning and chances are her day continued to be less than cheerful. However, she actually did have a choice. She could have laughed at how absurd the circumstances that occurred were (positive vibration). Even if she reacted badly to the first mishap (negative vibration), she could have caught herself, insisted – no, demanded – that she stop that kind of thinking, shaken it off and moved on with confidence that things would get better (positive vibration). I guarantee that her day would have turned out to be a bright one, even if the rain continued to pour.

The lesson here is that we're all the master of our own destiny. We're in control and we have the power to alter and change things. No one will come to our rescue because we are the rescuer ourselves. All of us do possess a free will, though, so we'll always be confronted with choices. When there's a fire we can either put it out or add fuel to it and let it burn. A good example of fuel here could be worry and anxiety. If we want to change our life, then we have to think positively and not let worry and anxiety get in the way because they're an absolute exercise in futility. If I could actually change something for the better by worrying then I would indeed be anxious day and night, but this is never the case. In fact, it does harm by wasting time when we could be moving into some sort of positive action. Worry and anxiety also take a negative toll on our physical health. Worst of all, worrisome thoughts put out vibrations that can actually bring about the things that worry us in the first place.

To be clear, when I talk about positive thinking, I don't by any means want any of us to be passive or naïve. Sometimes we need to place practicality, common sense and action behind positive thoughts. Something like, "Let me get all the information I need about these circumstances first and then decide what to do. I've been through this before and have mastered the situation. I can do it again." So, we're thinking positively but we're also taking responsibility for fixing things. That's putting out strong vibrations as well. There's always a solution. We just need to find it.

So, even what we think has energy behind it and causes vibrations that can attract what we want, keep undesirable things away from us, and create change which in turn can alter our entire destiny and bring about the personal and/or professional goals we desire.

* * *

We all eventually ask ourselves, "Am I really good enough?" It often triggers some uncomfortable feelings, but that's totally normal. From the very beginning of our lives, our parents and society have been telling us how we should be, what we should do and, in effect, what is right and wrong for us. They proclaim that they have the answers which hold the keys to our success. But we are unique individuals. One size does not fit all when we're talking about unique souls. Nevertheless, we aspired to being what everyone said we should be and that led us to be disconnected from ourselves because we could never fit that mold completely. This brain-washing has resulted in many of us feeling that we're not good enough as we are. We assume that we need to fit into some predetermined slot, but it's uncomfortable and causes anxiety. We know we need to change to be successful, but the only tools we're working with are what others say is good for us. I can say from personal experience that this never works. It's a shame, but it causes so many to hold themselves back and not use their full abilities.

To break through and unlock our full potential, we first need to make peace with our lack of self-confidence by recognizing its source in our early life. When we were born, we were 100% dependent on our parents and our environment.

Our family took care of us but they were also influencing us without our awareness, or perhaps even theirs. So, we shouldn't blame ourselves or them for problems that may have occurred because of this. They did their best but maybe they couldn't give us what we needed. It doesn't matter anymore, so we must just let go of it.

What's important is that when we find ourselves in the familiar situation of people or society still having expectations of us, we need to be really smart this time. We must ignore their expectations. We don't have to hate them, or tell them they're wrong. In fact, they usually have the best of intentions. We just need to realize that they have their opinions and we have ours. We are on our journey and they are on theirs. There's no competition here.

I knew someone that came from a very wealthy hotelier family. He was financially independent but felt empty, depressed and started to drink too much. Of course, he always found himself in terrible situations. Then he sought help and started to work on what he really, really wanted to do with his life. What he finally discovered was that flowers and trees were his passion. When he told his family that he wanted to open up a flower shop and become a landscaper, none of them understood. In fact, they were worried that he was throwing his future away and would be much better off being a "big" hotelier. "You're making the mistake of your life," they exclaimed. He eventually learned to ignore them and now owns a huge franchise company of flower shops. He's also happily married and has 2 children. This illustrates perfectly how we all can break the cycle of dependency and lead with our desires.

Another essential to success comes in understanding the limitations of our mind, because most of what it tells us is illusion. Instead, we should trust our intuition. When we meet someone, need to make a decision or are confronted with a situation that societal convention dictates are good for us, we need to listen to our body first. Do we have a lump in our throat when we speak with this person? Do we sweat when we're discussing this particular deal? Do we get a headache every time we think about this decision we must make? Remember, everything is about energy. Our body is sensitive and picks up all vibrations and invisible information as we walk our journey. It's sending us signs and signals all the time and when we listen to these messages, we do what is right for us. If we're experiencing discomfort, then we should walk away. We are here for a purpose and to live a life that brings us true peace and happiness.

I'll risk being repetitive here because I believe it's important to restate: We have been programmed to think that because the people we love or society taught us that we need to be a certain way or do certain things, then we have to. Nothing can be further from the truth. We don't have to do anything our intuition warns us against. It doesn't help us when we try to make other people happy at the risk of our own happiness. It's our journey. Only ours. We all need to be free from other people's expectations. The last breath we take will be our moment to reflect on our life. We'll realize that this was our voyage and we were responsible for the way we walked it. There won't be anyone there to judge us. We'll all be alone and what we do now will dictate whether we'll have regrets or will be content with the life we led.

So, are all of us good enough? Of course we are! We are god, we are unique, we are a creator. Everybody is special. We all need to open our eyes and realize that if we continue to say no to that question, we're probably using it as an excuse for not taking our chance. We are all perfect, and we have all the tools we need to discern information and use what's best for us. The universe is like someone whispering the winning numbers of the lottery in our ear. If we just fill out the form but don't bring it to the lottery vendor, we'll lose our chance. We have the tools but we must remind ourselves that we have them, and use them. Like that lottery, we have to be in it to win it.

We should all write this down: "I have the best shot at both personal and business success when I start to believe in my body, soul and emotions. We can trust our gut and move forward, in line with our intuition. Then we cannot go wrong. Peace, harmony and success on all levels of our lives will follow.

* * *

Before I end this chapter, I'd like to talk about the importance of being alone. Some might think that's strange at first, but I can testify that being alone bore many fruits that contributed to my success as an individual and business person. Let me explain.

Before we incarnated into our bodies, we were all connected as one with the universe. This was nice, but it didn't allow us to make our own experiences. Being here, in our own bodies, gives us the chance to be free individuals. When we spend time alone, we allow ourselves to connect with our soul and appreciate this individuality. Then we can make plans and decisions without the influence of others around us. We'll also be better able to discover what we really, really want.

Instead of trying to become one with someone else, or even worse, dependent upon another, it's important for us to accept that we're alone and when we're comfortable with that independence, we can then enjoy relationships with other people and loved ones unconditionally.

* * *

We all need to make a commitment here and now to take charge of our life and be the master of our destiny. We need to own that we are all responsible for our journey, that we have the power, that we can choose. We are each and one of us someone special, and everyone has the right to walk his or her own journey. We must stop saying, "No, I can't do that." I'll talk about developing and strengthening the tools we all need to achieve the success we desire in the chapters to come. The important thing now is that we all commit to stepping into our own power. Once we do that, the rest is a matter of practice.

Some things to think about...

Success in life, either personal or businesswise, can only happen when you pursue goals and dreams that are driven by what you love from your heart. Even if you're super intelligent and you have a masters from Harvard and everything is easy for you, if you're not truly happy with what you're doing – from the bottom of your heart – you won't make it. You're not a robot because your soul is spirit. Your mind is only a tool that you'll use to get to where you want to be.

IN THE STORM OF LIFE

But first you have to feel it, you have to find your passion. Ask yourself these questions:

1. What drives you? When are you most happy? What excites you?

2. What are your strengths? When the day is finished, are you more apt to have ideas? Or are you more inspired in the morning? Are you a visionary, are you a philosopher? Are you practical and precise, are you mechanical or are you a creative? Are you comfortable as a leader or more contented to be a team player?

3. Look for the thread that ties your strengths with things that make you happy. Start jotting them down to see if they direct you to setting certain goals for yourself.

4. Let's dig a little deeper. What would you do if you were financially independent? What would you change in your life or career? Did you always want to study acting, writing or engineering but financial circumstances got in the way? Would you chase those careers if money weren't an issue now? Do you want to be in a position of power? Or perhaps you possess a lot of empathy and would pursue humanitarian causes to make a grand change in the world?

5. After giving these some thought, did you make new goals? If so, write them down. That's the first step toward manifestation. I often

seal this process with the sentence in my head, "This is the first day of my new life."

6. Now start focusing on your goals. Use your energy to concentrate on what you desire. By the way, if you're feeling a little bit of anxiety you might be picking up the energy from other people who perhaps don't think your goals are attainable. Or it might just be your old beliefs popping up. We'll talk about dealing with fear and anxiety in the next chapter, but for now just acknowledge them. They will pass.

When you really know what you want, then your journey begins. Your vibration will change and you can start to use the power of visualization which we'll talk about in detail in another chapter. Start acting and living as though you've already achieved your goals. Your energy will be connected to the universal mind and your thoughts will materialize into reality. It's like changing the frequency of your radio channel and dialing into the right station. You were on Hip Hop and now you're on Classical Music. Whatever is right for you, you'll choose your channel and that will be the rocket that catapults you to reaching your goal. You're on a journey and you've chosen your destination. Now you need to choose your flight.

THE ILLUSION OF FEAR

WHEN FRANKLIN D. ROOSEVELT UTTERED THOSE FAMOUS words, "The only thing we have to fear is fear itself," he was talking about the very real threat that war was presenting to the world. Still, I don't completely agree with what he said. For me, fear is not something of which we should be afraid. Fear is actually our friend and wants to show us something really important. Let me explain. Fear is a signal that always alerts us to the fact that something significant is happening. Viewing it that way, fear was telling the world that it needed to pay attention and take action that early December day in 1941.

Another example of how fear is our friend can be seen in the way our bodies react when we're in real danger of physical harm. Our heart beat begins to race and we start to perspire – all ways in which our bodies are preparing us to flee from danger. Sort of the way we would rev up a car to escape a dangerous situation quickly.

So, fear should never be dreaded, or ignored, for that matter. The brand of fear I'd like to focus in on this chapter, however, is not the kind that occurs when we're staring down the barrel of a gun or walking in a dangerous neighborhood. Instead, I'd like to explore the sort of fear we experience when we're confronted with a career change, trying to lose weight or need to leave an unhappy relationship. Why are we so afraid of these feelings? So many of us will run away, hide, pray – do anything to avoid experiencing these emotions. However, fear is not the enemy. It's never the problem. Fear can indeed be our best friend, but we often misread it badly and don't take advantage of what it's telling us.

As with all things, we learned this habit from our earliest years here on earth. When we're born, we're totally dependent upon our parents. We're new to our bodies in a world that we perceive as too big and often times scary. We therefore believe everything our parents tell us. In fact, we hang onto every word they say because that's the only way we feel we can survive in this seemingly cold world. We're so little and new to the earth.

The problem is that we hold on to these fears as we become adults. We're always looking for mom, dad, wife, husband or boss to protect us and show us the way. We forgot that we actually came to this earth with a plan. In fact, our souls chose the exact life we're living before we incarnated – with the full cast of characters with whom we play out our lives. What's more, we actually selected our strengths and weaknesses, both emotionally and physically, before we got here. In addition, we decided on the purpose for which we incarnated and indeed wanted to fulfill all the particular tasks needed to reach our ultimate goals.

The obvious question then becomes, "Why do we react with fear to circumstances that were pre-chosen by us in the first place?" The short answer to that is we forgot. When a baby is first born, he's extremely charismatic because he's newly incarnated and hasn't been affected by worldly circumstances. He is still "of the universe," so to speak. That soon changes when his parents and the outside world in general begin to teach him what it is he should do, want and fear. That's when the first feeling of being alone arises.

As he grows, he becomes more and more disconnected from his own, true feelings and eventually doesn't have a clue as to what's going on inside himself. He loses the ability to feel the intense emotions he first experienced as a child because he's learned to not feel. For example, when a child cries, a parent will rarely if ever say, "It's okay, I am here for you. You can cry. I feel with you. Cry because that's what you're feeling." No, instead the parent is more likely to say, "Don't cry. Please don't cry." After a while, the child begins to internalize this and eventually believes that his experiences are not important at all. He thinks that he simply cannot be in touch with his inner feelings because that will also bring him to tears and that is not welcomed. Children experience feelings that can range from deeply exciting to extremely sad and fearful. It's natural for them, but even expressing positive emotions is just not welcomed in our world. So, the child learns and then truly believes that he must never do that again. This is the exact moment he becomes profoundly disconnected from his emotions and therefore his inner self.

The child also becomes so dependent upon his parents to survive that he views them as the entire outside world. He focuses mainly on their moods, wondering when would be a good time to ask for something and when it would be better to remain silent and avoid them. When he grows into adulthood, the disconnection from his inner world continues. The only change is that the "real" outside world replaces his parents. So now, instead of focusing on Mom and Dad he focuses on this outside world which he views as frightening most of the time. This is the foundation on which he's building his life and it leads to his becoming lost, empty and void of vibrance. He fears almost everything.

To compound it all, he begins to use his mind to analyze what the real truth is. He concludes that he could never really live up to all that society (the outside world) expects of him and begins to feel that he's not good enough. He hears society barking in his ear, "Don't feel this – you need to change to be successful!" Everywhere he goes and in everything he encounters, society continues to clamor, "Behave yourself and don't do that or I promise, you'll fail!" In effect, society has taken the place of his parents.

So now this once vibrant, loving, feeling child learns that as an adult he cannot live openly, as he is. He needs to be "smart" and adopt to the rules of society. He continues to live disconnected from himself and the nagging notion of not being good enough becomes his daily companion. So, it's no wonder that when he faces a challenge, fear pops up immediately. We have all experienced this to one degree or another in our lives. It's important to remember, though, that we're never really afraid of what will happen. Instead, we're mostly scared of the hidden emotions behind the fear. We just never want to feel them or accept any of it about ourselves. We therefore feel trapped and don't see how we can set ourselves free and unlock our full potential.

These emotions that we don't want to feel about ourselves are almost always the same. In fact, I would confidently say that most people are challenged with one or two of them. The following list are feelings with which so many of us can identify...

Powerlessness
Helplessness
Guilt
Inferiority
Loneliness
Grief
Shame

Of course, we could opt to just live with these fears (hidden emotions) and get by as best we can. However, we're not here to just survive. Instead, we came here to create experiences and fulfill our personal purpose. Again, we must keep in mind that before we incarnated, we knew the bigger meaning of our lives and all the tools we would possess upon this earth. We've just forgotten our power, wisdom and yes, endlessness.

For many people, the first step to unlocking their full potential is to make peace with these hidden, deep-rooted emotions within themselves. We can all benefit by doing that. As soon as we own who we really are and also accept our feelings of being alone or not good enough, we'll find that we don't need to hide them anymore. That's when we'll step into our real power and set ourselves free. We'll begin to sense more energy arise in our soul and body and we'll immediately start focusing on what we really, really want to do with our life. Fear is our friend, a guide to show us how to look at these hidden emotions and accept them. It offers us the possibility of setting ourselves free from fear-based behavior and thinking.

Now that we're ready to discover, live and express our true purpose, we'll become successful and find the job or personal goal for which we're longing. We'll finally be in control of our own life. We'll be free and become the creator of our destiny instead being trapped and a victim of our anxiety. The feeling of power and joy when all the fear disappears is an experience that cannot be expressed in words. One needs to feel it to understand it. It can happen for each and every one of us.

* * *

At this point, I'd like to talk about transformation as it relates to the phenomenon of Dualism. As an illustration, let's talk about a businessman who always becomes upset and even worse, aggressive, when deals don't turn out as he expected or fall through completely. He becomes afraid that he might fail and that puts a lot of pressure on him. The fact is, his stress and fear are actually connected to an inner emotion, with which he has yet to make peace. The inner emotion here is most likely his feeling of powerlessness. In addition, he views himself as isolated because he's the one who is carrying so much of the responsibility all of the time and all by himself. What he doesn't realize is that he's actually here in this lifetime to experience power and connectedness.

So, what does he need to do to change the habit of reacting to obstacles in this manner? He actually has to allow himself to be powerless. When he does that, he'll become whole. As dualism is the foundation of life, he'll live fulfilled by being powerless at times, yet still love and accept himself as he is. Then he'll enjoy being powerful all the more when his business dealings turn out to be successful and highly profitable. It's important to remember here that his self-value and self-respect would never be dependent on his successes, per se. Our businessman would just create his experiences around power and powerlessness without judging any of them and enjoy his life.

So, life is based on dualism. The journey we choose for ourselves therefore always begins at the opposite side of what we want to learn and experience in this life. For example, when someone comes here to discover power and strength then this person will definitely choose a family where he'll feel weak, lonely and lost. There are many circumstances that might cause him to experience these feelings. Perhaps his parents are successful, wealthy business people and don't really look to connect with the child because they're too busy and have a nanny to attend to him. They don't encourage him to strive because they're rich and know that he'll inherit it all anyway. So, this child doesn't have the chance to show how strong he is or what kind of leader he could be. This will result in his always being scared when he's faced with authority or successful people because he'll always be challenged with a lack of self-confidence.

The good news is that even though this man's fear of not being strong and smart enough will reoccur time and again, that same fear will eventually push him to the point where he cannot avoid who he really is any longer. He'll finally accept his lack of self-confidence and realize that what makes him the most afraid is what would fulfill him the most. That's when he'll be completely free and understand that with the burden of fear off his shoulders, he can now break through and step into his own life and purpose.

I'm no stranger to this kind of fear and dualism. For example, I go on speaking engagements a lot. Of course, like so many people, I have a fear of public speaking. Before I step on stage, I make peace with my lack of self-confidence. Then I walk on stage and come across as being very natural. I've experienced this time and time again and as a result I've discovered that this is what my biggest passion is – to be on stage and speaking to my audience.

We must all approach our fears this way. If not, we would only exist and stop living. We would also become depressed and lose energy – both physically and spiritually. That's not an alternative for anyone. I've noticed how sometimes a grave illness gives people the opportunity to wake up and motivate themselves to break through to something really important, even if it's extremely challenging. Why have so many of the most successful, wealthy people in the history of our world faced such adversity in their lives? I would venture to say that more than half of them found themselves bankrupt at least one time in their careers. In fact, they all endured many failures and hardships until they finally succeeded. That's what Dualism is all about. Fear offers us the chance to transform and to see who we really are.

It's a basic truth that we all need to realize: To come back to ourselves and become whole, we need to remember that we're here for a purpose. How can we jolt our universal memory? We need to observe the experiences in our life and note the consistencies. People and places might change, but we're always creating experiences of one type of another that weave the fabric of our story. We'll come to realize that everyone we've walked with on this journey was here with us for a reason. The older we get, the more we'll see that the frame was set from the very beginning and that our life is a fascinating book that was actually prewritten even though we have free will of choice. That's one of the best things about getting older, because when we're young we don't see what I call the "Bigger Picture of Our Lives." We all eventually learn to see the purposes of our lives and it all begins to make perfect sense.

This would be the perfect time for us to reexamine the seven emotions we listed a few pages back. If any one of them really affects us, then we must identify it, own it and most off all make our peace with it. We need to know and believe that the opposite of that emotion is that for which we came here. It's crucial to understand that the fear is just an illusion. That's when we'll really begin to enjoy our journey.

* * *

In summary, the things we want most will always scare us the most. It's Dualism and that's the way life works. However, if we just take that first step and walk through the fear and anxiety – accepting them for the illusions they are – then we can come to terms with the emotion behind that which frightens us. We'll no longer avoid feeling, and making peace with it will result in our becoming "Our Authentic Selves." Then and only then will we succeed and be able to live a fulfilled life.

It's good to remember that although we used the business man as an example, this also applies to personal success, like finding the right life partner, city in which to live or even hobbies. We cannot have one without the other; we must have personal happiness to have professional fulfillment. There must be the balance.

We must also remember that we didn't come here to just survive. Instead, we came here for a higher purpose. We shouldn't try so hard to conquer our fears and control and manage the challenges in our life. We need to accept them and watch how they pass away. Nothing happens by accident – it's always meant to be. We'll see that we're never really in danger when these fears rear their ugly heads. Instead, we're protected by the immense power from which we were created. We are part of it.

Some things to think about...

Find yourself a comfortable spot – at home, in the park, on the beach – and ask yourself the following questions. For me, it's best to be alone. The silence may even answer the questions for you. Jot them down as they come to you. You can always go back and change your answers if your soul speaks to you later on with different responses.

- Which experience(s) do you think your soul chose for you to create?

- What circumstances upset you and really get under your skin?

- Remember, there are two sides to every coin. So now write down what empowers you most.

- Where can you identify the connectedness?

- Now think about your fears. You might get a little anxious, but just walk through it. The anxiety will pass.

- What scares you the most?
- What would you do in life if you were fearless?

LIFE IS NEVER LOGICAL

WITH ALL THAT WE'VE EXPERIENCED IN JUST living throughout the years, most of us would agree that life is not logical. However, to really examine whether or not that's true, we must first clearly define "logical." When we use our minds to try and figure it out, that's where problems arise.

I do believe that life is not logical. But I also know that we cannot analyze why this is so. The moment we use our brain to try to make sense of it all, we make a mistake because we can't "think" or "explain" our life mentally. We can only live our life emotionally – in all of its illogical wonder.

Within the scope of the universal truths of life, our minds are limited. Our emotions, however, our boundless. While our brains continually try to find answers to the "why's" in life (logic), our emotions effortlessly discover the wonders, joys and answers to the mysteries of life. That's why it's so crucial that we be closely connected to our emotions.

It's important to note that our emotions also play a practical role in guiding us through our journeys here on earth. If we pay close attention, our emotions will show us the paths which eventually unfold the very opportunities for which we are longing. In other words, our emotions are a gift that acts as a door to life itself.

Of course, our brain serves many functions, like balancing our checkbooks and such. However, it can't help us experience life. When we try to live with our thoughts instead of our emotions – when we constantly analyze what is happening instead of feeling and embracing it – we become disconnected from ourselves. We feel as though we are existing but not truly living, and this can very often lead to mental illnesses such as depression, addiction or at the very least, burnout.

In order to live a fulfilled life, we need to stop trying to find the logic in life. We should utilize our emotions and that's when we'll discover that life is indeed supposed to be illogical. That's what makes it such a miracle.

* * *

Now, while we should pay less attention to our mind when trying to navigate our life, I recommend we all pay very close attention to our body. In fact, our body is there to communicate with our emotions and that's so valuable. We can always count on our body to help us discern what's really going on emotionally and it indeed becomes an invaluable tool when making decisions that can alter the rest of our life.

For instance, let's say Edward is in a meeting that is very important to his business future. He'll need to make imperative decisions based on this meeting, but his brain will be very little help because it will only try to calculate the outcome when it has no resources to do so. Here's where Edward's emotions-body connection can really assist him. If everything that happened in the meeting went fine (or so his mind says) but when he left, he felt empty or irritated, then he needs to stop and reflect. Even if there's no logic to it, his body is telling him that this may not be the right thing for him. I often talk about listening to our gut, no matter how right the numbers and logic seem. Our gut is ALWAYS right.

Of course, this applies to personal matters, as well. Elaine might be involved with a man that everyone says is wrong for her. Nevertheless, every time she's with him she feels both elated and calm, all at the same time. Why don't people like the man for Elaine? Maybe he's a widower with five kids and her friends and family feel she'll be taking on too much. It doesn't matter. If Elaine feels good when she's with him, then she should move forward with the relationship.

The point is, we have our body to create experiences for us. After all, our body houses our soul and this intimate relationship between body and soul is important for us to understand. We're so much more than we think or see when we look in the mirror. Our attractive faces and fit bodies are only here to carry our souls, which are infinite and possess their source and energy in the universe. Our soul therefore has the ability to connect us with the infinite universe via our thoughts and even more so with our emotions. As I said in Chapter 1, we vibrate and that means that we are energy itself. Because our souls are attached to our bodies, we can use our bodies to take signals from the energy of the universe and create our own experiences through decision making and taking action.

So, we should think of our body as a conduit through which our emotions send signals to lead us to the right paths in our life. Because we're human beings, our emotions can only guide us. It's our body that must actually make things happen. We must never forget, though, that emotions are our source, our heartbeat. We live and decide through our emotions alone.

* * *

Our relationship with emotions is a funny thing. We either want to experience them with great enthusiasm, or avoid them at any cost. There's no in between. But it's important to realize that all of our desires are connected to particular emotions that we long to experience. The guy who wants to buy an expensive car thinks that's his heart's desire. In reality, he really wants to experience the emotion of self-confidence, especially when he shows the new car to friends and colleagues and sees how impressed they are. Self-confidence is the feeling for which he is looking.

When a woman wants to travel alone with only a backpack through India, what she really desires are the emotions of freedom, self-sufficiency and power that embarking on such an adventure will bring her. A couple, on the other hand, might want to buy a house with a big garden – quite a contrast to the traveling woman. What the couple really desires, though, are the emotions of security and connectedness that living together as a family will provide them.

Our fears work similarly in that things we don't desire also carry emotions with them. These emotions, however, are ones that trigger uncomfortable feelings, so we do everything we can to steer clear of them. This is where we make a mistake. We believe that to be more efficient and successful in this life, we must control our emotions. To be clearer, we let the good emotions run wild but we try to put a chokehold on the perceived bad emotions. It's really quite impossible, though. We just end up postponing them and when they do show up again, they're often more intense and quite chaotic.

I really don't believe that any emotions are bad. If our emotions are connected to the universal oneness then how could any one of them be wrong for us? They are there to send signals to our bodies to prompt us to move, to do something, to create an experience. When the emotion is uncomfortable, it is surely telling us to either stay clear of a situation or to go at full force because it will bring about change that will eventually lead to good things. But we need to experience it. That's why I always say that fear is most often our friend.

It's important to remember that we cannot experience only one side of our feelings. Because life is based on Dualism, we will always have to experience both sides. There will always be both day and night and there is nothing to judge about it. We just need to live it. When we connect to our emotions, we can feel them like waves and then even the ones we don't like become an experience. Nothing more...nothing less.

So, to control our emotions by ignoring them is like committing suicide. Not literally, of course, but certainly spiritually. When we ignore the emotions that come from our soul – which is part of the universal energy of existence – we stop living, we stop experiencing life, and we become robots. This is a sure-fire road to failure, and that is what we were so fearful of in the first place.

Some things to think about...

Now, of course, everything we discussed in this chapter assumes that you are in touch with your emotions. Unfortunately, many people are disconnected from them. They continue to analyze situations with their brains but don't really know how they truly feel about anything. These folks are really missing the essence of life.

Does this sound like you? If so, the following are some exercises that will help you learn to be in touch with your emotions, no matter how painful they seem at first. Once you do that, you can then work on trying not to suppress them or ignore them completely. Then your life becomes complete, you are free from whatever happens and you will start to enjoy everything.

Before asking yourself the following questions, remember that you also can truly influence what happens in your life through your emotions. You can attract beautiful situations, events and people because same attracts same. That is to say, the same energy level and frequency attracts that which vibrates on the same energy level and frequency. What's really powerful is that you can decide on which frequency you want to be because you are the master of your life and destiny.

It's time to examine what's behind your actions and discover the emotions for which you are longing and perhaps even more importantly, those of which you are fearful. The idea is to embrace all of them. That's when you'll understand the bigger picture and then you can make informed decisions by being honest and accepting you for whom you are so you can reach the goals and success you desire.

Ask yourself:

- What I am really afraid of? Being powerless, lonely or disrespected?

- For which emotions am I longing? Safety, recognition, connectedness, love?

- Are my desires in line with what I really want? Or am I influenced by the expectations of others – my family, friends or the society in which I live?

- Who am I? How do I define myself, in terms of my personality and soul?

Some more questions I actually can help you answer:

- Do you have a lack of self-confidence? If so, then just accept it.

- Do you feel alone? Actually, you are alone. You came alone and you go alone and you live alone in your body. That is bliss because you can "feel" other people. Remember, we were all connected in that place from where we all came. The boundary of our bodies now allows us to make our own experiences. Own it and be free.

As soon as you accept who you are and understand the miracle of life – that all is out of energy and permanently moving – you'll become aware that life is not logical. You can then start making experiences and feel them. You'll embrace yourself, be free and more unique, and begin to really enjoy your life. You're here for a reason and you have a purpose. Celebrate it.

WHY WE NEED TO BE ALONE

MANY PEOPLE ARE TERRIFIED OF BEING ALONE. Some, for example, will stay in an unhealthy and even abusive relationship instead of living by themselves. What they're really scared of, however, isn't being alone. It's more about having to face what's actually going on inside themselves, without the distraction of another person in the house.

Part of the problem is a result of the society in which we live. To put it plainly, we're never left alone with our thoughts. There always seems to be a TV or a video streaming in waiting areas, in taxis and even in public toilets. Noise is everywhere and accompanies us wherever we go. If it's not there, then we create it. We walk with ear buds playing music or podcasts. We even take our obsession for distracting noise home with us. Indeed, many people can't cook, clean or do their work unless the TV or radio are on, even if in the distance. It's quite frankly made us all scared of silence.

It wouldn't be so bad if we were actually entertained by all the clamor. In these situations, the noise gives us little solace or enjoyment. We somehow still seem to feel disconnected and lonely. Nevertheless, we avoid silent spaces because we're simply not use to them and they frighten us so much.

Again, it's not the silence that's instilling such fear in us. Instead, we subconsciously know that if there were nothing to distract us, we'd have to face what we are feeling and deal with our emotions. As we said in the previous chapter, avoiding emotions is one of the biggest errors we can make in life. Even if what we're feeling is different than what our minds are wishing or hoping for, we still need to deal with these emotions or we'll forever be lost.

Just like the song, "The Sound of Silence," quietness does in fact speak volumes. It affords us the opportunity to reconnect with ourselves and our deeper being. We're so much more than we think we are in the scheme of our lifetime and yes, in the vast universe, but we lost the connection to our soul and profound existence.

The universal truth is that allowing ourselves to be alone, and better yet in silence at times, magically and mystically reconnects us to the higher being we were (and still are) before we incarnated and walked this earth. It also connects us to other souls and beings. This is crucial to helping us understand the bigger picture and finding the right paths in our life. I, for one, don't make a move without first spending a significant amount of time alone to listen to what my higher being is telling me.

Before we incarnated into our bodies, we were all energy, light and limitlessness. There was no friction, no obstacle, no unclarity. There was also no way to make a mistake because we were part of the universal truth, with nothing to distract us. Truth was truth, and we were united to it so much so that it was a part of us. The only downside to this was that because we were one with the energy and vibration of the universe – and one with the other souls that shared that same vibration – there was no opportunity for uniqueness. No way for personal, creative expression. That's why we incarnated. We needed our bodies to create our own experiences, make our own, individual mark on life, and experience our own being by going on our own journey.

What's more, before we got here, we already decided what we wanted to accomplish on this particular earth's journey. The universe helped us along by giving us choices, such as who our parents would be and who were to be our partners and friends to accompany us along the journey. We also chose things like our nationality, religion, race, country, gender, appearance and body constitution. We selected carefully and wisely, based on the particular experiences we wanted to have.

I understand this well because with the help of a professional, hypnotic coach I travelled through many of my past lives for one year. I was completely present in these lives and the different situations I encountered. Indeed, I could even feel, smell and touch things during my visits to those past lives. I also learned so much from my travels. For one, I completely and finally understood that there is no time. I now know that all of my lives are actually happening simultaneously, in a parallel fashion. Of course, this is hard to fathom when we attempt to use our mind to analyze it. That is far beyond our brains' comprehension.

I also became acutely aware of the fact that the very situations I experienced and am still living through in this present life – and the people with whom I find myself – are not arbitrary. It all happens for a reason, and I chose that reason before I got here. I arranged it all. Understanding this gave me a great sense of empowerment because I actually masterminded my life. No matter what happened – or will happen – can only be for good because I chose it and I certainly wouldn't opt for anything bad to happen to me. In addition, I realized that I chose this journey to have the opportunity to learn something from it. Of course, it's up to me whether or not I still want to do anything on my journey, since we always have free choice.

Of course, my mind tries to muddle things at times. It often tries to convince me that I am perhaps a victim of unfortunate circumstances or that I made a bad mistake. When that occurs, I find a quiet place to reconnect with my higher being – the one that made all of these very wise decisions for me – and listen. And trust.

Our mind may be brilliant but it is no match for our soul, whose knowledge is universal and limitless. That's why it's so important to find time alone to hear what our soul is telling us. It will never let us down.

* * *

Of course, there are times when things happen suddenly and we can't just run into a room and close the door to be alone and listen to our soul speak. Our soul knows that, so it equipped us with intuition and gut feelings – a way to speak to us amid the noise and clamor of our daily life, when quiet time is just not an option.

We've touched upon this in the last chapter but it bears repeating. When we walk into a home or meet a person and we either feel cozy and attracted or scared and irritated, we can trust these reactions. We might very well have been in that place before and the circumstances were not ideal. In effect, we're picking up the energy and memories from a past life and we're being urged to heed the green or red light, depending on the situation. Of course, we don't understand exactly what's going on because in this current life we're experiencing the situation for the first time. Our brain doesn't need to comprehend any of it. In fact, it can't. We just need to use the vibrations and energy we share with the universe – which are in effect tools – and go with our intuition. If we make this a habit we just can't go wrong.

Indeed, gut and intuition are great instruments when a decision-making situation arises all of the sudden and we can't be alone to listen to our soul's advice. Like all instruments, though, they require upkeep. So, we still need time alone to reconnect with our universal soul to hone our gut instincts and fine-tune our intuition. It's just like recharging a battery.

It's also very important to remember that closely tied to our gut and intuition are emotions. When we do the work and reconnect with our emotions, the world will open up to us. We'll be empowered to live the life for which we came here. The real challenge is society, which has taught us to control or suppress our emotions. But that only disconnects us from our bigger and higher being, which often leads us to feeling lost and isolated. We then feel as though we're just existing but not really living, because life comes to us only through our feelings and we're repressing them.

What do we do when this happens? Our minds are limited and can't comprehend the power we truly possess through our emotions. So, we must not attempt to figure this out using mental processes. The answer is, of course, the subject of this chapter and can't be repeated enough: We have to find time alone to connect with our emotions. We'll learn to live more of our potential, go deeper and feel deeper. We'll discover the purpose of the life we chose and will learn to enjoy it with all its faces and all its ups and downs. We'll connect with our universal existence and the whole, huge being that is us.

Given all of this, sometimes we might feel that our body seems to be getting in the way. Really, it's not. We must remember that we need our body to execute our journey. Also, our body allows us to live and feel what it means to forgive or to love, to lose, to let go, to receive or to be powerful. For sure, we chose to come here to experience some if not all of those things. Most politicians, for example – especially the really important ones – incarnated to experience power. There's nothing wrong with that. There's no good or bad about any of it. They're all just experiences. I'll talk about the illusion of judgement later in this book, but for now we need to realize that we must not judge – especially ourselves – what emotions we have or experiences for which we are longing.

So, we should not be so hard on our body. I think of our body in terms of ice cubes and our soul in terms of water – it's all about form. As long as an ice cube stays in its form and the temperature allows it to do so, it is unique to itself with its own particular shape. However, when the temperature changes and the cube melts away, it doesn't stop existing; it just changes its form and becomes water. So, when we liken our bodies to ice cubes and our souls to water, then we see that there is no need to fear death because we are only changing form. Our spirit, our consciousness and our soul will keep living and flowing, just like water. It is indeed limitless.

* * *

What are some of the other benefits to connecting with our higher soul and emotions when we utilize being alone? For one, when we reconnect to the whole universe, we have this intense feeling of safety. We just know we're not in danger. That's because this higher level of consciousness guides and protects us through our journey – the one we chose in the first place. So, in effect, being alone teaches us that we're not really alone after all. You can find in this loneliness a profound stillness. Infinity is in the gap between your thoughts and your busy mind.

Therefore, we all need to step into our own silence. There we can find our true self when we allow ourselves to be alone and listen. It's true that many of us feel as though we're on a dangerous path and need to fight to survive. However, that changes the minute we go deep inside and change our focus. We'll then discover that the perilous challenges, irritation, games and losses are all on the periphery of our life. We'll see with such clarity that deep and center are our truth, our purpose, our real power, our infinite soul and our connectedness to the whole. That's why Buddha smiled when he became enlightened. He finally understood the bigger meaning and stopped sweating the details. He knew that we're here to create our own experiences – not just to survive.

Some things to think about...

You are now learning to be meditative, silent, totally present and universally aware. You'll remain authentic to your true self and at the same time live your vibrant life to the fullest.

When you let go of dealing with things that live only on the surface of your life and start engaging with what's truly going on inside yourself in every single situation, you'll triumphantly step into this true self and infinite power. Only one step is necessary: Accept that you are alone. To be able to live your purpose, you need to be alone in your body.

To reconnect to yourself, you can use the following exercise. Try not to get distracted. If intrusive thoughts pop into your head, change your focus and oust them from your mind. Really, truly feel what is going on inside yourself.

- Lay down on a yoga mat, with your head on a small pillow.

- Give yourself a moment and start to take steady, deep breaths.

- Inhale deeply, keep the breath in for a few seconds, then slowly exhale.

- Reflect in the silence and ask yourself, "What am I feeling at this exact moment? How does this emotion(s) make me feel? Where I am feeling it?

- Stay in the emotions and just feel them. Don't try to change them. Just accept them as they are. Accept yourself while feeling like this, as well.

Repeat this exercise for 10 minutes every day, or every other day. If you don't have a diary, perhaps this would be a good time to get one, ask yourself the following questions and make notes...

- Do I feel a particular way during the week and differently during the weekends?

- When I allow myself to connect with my emotions, do I consistently feel tense in one particular organ or part in my body? Where is that located and how does it feel?

- What happens when I continue to breathe and allow the pain to be?

- How does it feel when I accept that everything is what is it is, and it's all right to let it be that way?

- When I repeat the affirmation "I AM," how does that make me feel?

When you continue with the exercise and are familiar with it, you will become aware of yourself. You'll be "present" all the time – in your office before and during a meeting, while traveling or while sitting in a tub. Even if you're on a first date or find yourself in a stressful situation or environment, you'll act outside and stay centered in what is going on inside yourself.

Remember...reconnect, breathe with awareness and feel what's going on inside you without trying to change anything. You came here for a reason and have chosen your purpose. You are an amazing, powerful soul. When you stay centered, you'll feel your true power and the bigger meaning of your life will become apparent in every single moment of every single day of your existence.

THE TRUTH ABOUT DUALISM

I'M SURE WE ALL AGREE THAT THERE are two sides to every story. If so, then why do we tend to stick with only one side most of the times? And that one side is always the easiest for us to accept. It's usually the scenario that makes us feel good about ourselves and instills in us a sense of self-confidence. After all, everyone wants to feel happy, be successful and have harmonious partnerships. But then there are those other sides of life. Feeling badly, failure and broken relationships – those are the ones that we want to ignore or even refuse to accept.

The thing about focusing solely on the positive sides of life is that we end up missing so many experiences that we're meant to feel. We're not here only to have good times. No one is immune to setbacks, challenges and arguments because we're not supposed to be. The reality is, life is not one-sided. Its structure, truth and philosophy are based on Dualism. We're here to experience it all.

Dualism is a gift and is indeed an intrinsic part of life, which is beautiful. The problem lies in the way we react to it. We tend to make Dualism more complicated than it is because we're consistently judging both sides of life. One person may love the daylight and dislike nighttime. Another might prefer sunshine to rain. I know these are simplistic examples, but they really do illustrate the point. What's wrong with the darkness of night or a downpour of rain now and then? Day and night, sunshine and rain...neither is inherently good nor bad. They're just on opposite sides of a spectrum and happen all the time. We should never try to judge or avoid either side because the consequence will lead to suffering when there's no actually reason for it.

So, everything in life is based on Dualism, and if we would just respect that truth and go with the flow, we'd be in a much better place most of the time. However, the problem starts when we evaluate and give priority to one aspect of life and discount the other. When we do this, we're only accepting half of life instead of fully embracing the whole of it.

So, why is life based on Dualism? In traveling through my other lives, I learned that the main purpose of incarnating is almost always not just to be successful. Instead, we come here to create and feel experiences. If our purpose was to possess power, be free, or have connectedness and love, then we chose to experience the polar opposites of those emotions. In other words, Dualism.

For example, if a soul decides to incarnate in order to become a powerful person, he selects parents and partners who keep him small and decide everything for him, instead of helping him to step into his own power. He therefore feels safe with giving up his power to others and it therefore scares him to make his own decisions. However, as soon as he faces the things he doesn't like and steps into his power, he discovers what fulfills him most and is therefore free because he now can accept and embrace both sides. So, when he reconnects with whom he really is, he can finally accept being both powerless and powerful and in doing so, will become whole.

As another example, if someone wants to incarnate in order to experience freedom, she will choose parents and partners who are overprotective. Conflict arises because she prefers to live in security and is therefore afraid of taking risks and being adventurous. However, when she faces her fears, she finds that freedom is her biggest fulfillment. That's when she is free and can enjoy both sides of the story, as we can never have one side alone. The point is to accept what we don't like and actual be afraid of it because in doing so, our real life starts as we're enjoying both sides. As for our conflicted friend, as soon as she changes her focus, looks inside and totally accepts both sides of her existence, she'll discover that the biggest joy in life is to experience both freedom and security.

It's the same with the emotions of connectedness and loneliness. When people focus on the outside, they fixate on loneliness and do everything they can not to be alone. However, when they, for example, are at home alone one evening and allow that emotion to come up, after a while something changes inside. It's like an inner opening because the person doesn't reject that emotion anymore and as a result starts to enjoy being alone. That's when they are able to love and embrace both sides – connectedness and loneliness. Again, we can never have only one side.

Many people struggle with Dualism. They need to learn how to embrace both sides of every aspect of their lives, never letting themselves be sad about the bad, empty or lonely times. They should just let them happen and most importantly, truly feel and live them. When these folks modify their behavior and stop trying to change either side of life, they inevitably experience something deep and wonderful, where huge burdens have been lifted off their shoulders.

When we stop judging the different sides of life as being good or bad, and fully live both the ups and downs of our existence, we'll be able to open up to life fully. We'll walk in peace, permitting life to be just as it is. There is only one step necessary to allowing our emotions to be: we need to feel and not judge. In doing so, then another level opens up and we're able to enjoy both sides and all the emotions that come with them. The point is that we have to go beyond the emotions because they're never as bad as we think they might be. As a matter of fact, they are extremely important to us. Remember, we can NEVER experience only one side. So, in order live fulfilled we have to let both sides come and go without judgement.

Life is like a pendulum; it goes this way, then that way, and then swings back again. We just need to let it flow instead of trying to hang onto only one side because that's when we create pain and suffering for ourselves. My coach, for example, was at a stage in his life where he was not able to pay his rent. When the landlord knocked angrily at his door, he just kept writing his book and allowed his emotions of powerlessness to arise. Then things changed. He became free and after being powerless he stepped into his power, picked up the phone and made a deal with the landlord. He became really powerful because he allowed himself to feel powerlessness. These emotions are his purpose and that's why he incarnated.

* * *

There's really no mystery to accepting the Dualism of life. However, acceptance doesn't mean that we're powerless to create change. To the contrary, we have the awesome power to alter anything and everything because we were created with that ability. The thing to remember is that we must make changes within ourselves first.

Therefore, we need to discover the power and tools to change things deep inside us. When we desire to shift something in our life, we have to make internal shifts first. This does take a bit of discipline because of the society in which we live. Commercialism teaches us to focus only on material things outside ourselves. It conditions us to chase after items we believe we must have, places we think we need to be and businesses we're convinced will make us successful. That's a lot of energy to exert. It would be better to use our momentum to examine what's going on deep within us and make necessary shifts so that we can be equipped to create the changes we want in order to be successful. The material things we desire will be attracted to our inner shift and appear, because same attracts the same. Everything is energy, life force and experience. We don't need to own what we desire. We just need to experience it.

When we think about what has happened to us on our life's journey thus far, most of see a path that has led us to failure, then success, then failure again, and so on. We might think there has been no sense to it. Well, when we only celebrate the successes and mourn the losses, then there is no sense because we won't reach our desired goals. However, if we accept the fact that life is full of good times and the difficult ones as well – because it's based on a foundation of Dualism – then we'll learn to enjoy and accept both the failures and successes. We'll see the bigger picture. Our burdens will disappear and we'll become a magnet for success or whatever we want to achieve in our lives.

* * *

When we talk about the dangers of only chasing what we perceive as "good," we're in no way saying that we don't want to enjoy the luxurious possessions that success and wealth can afford us. What we are saying is that we'll be happier and more fulfilled if we change our focus to living each side of life with all of our emotions. When we let life happen, we'll start seeing the bigger picture of our purpose and will be able to enjoy it all.

There are people who find many aspects of life's Dualism challenging. Love and hate, sadness and happiness, light and dark, power and powerlessness. We've all experienced them, and we sometimes toiled over the "negative" ones. However, we need to start learning not to stigmatize what seems less desirable with a stamp of disapproval. We should make a commitment now to live life authentically by accepting the whole of it – each side equally. It will be easy because we'll find that quiet, alone space we talked about in the last chapter, and will start to connect with what's going on within our soul. We'll begin to see that life happens inside of us, not outside. Actually, everything which is outside started inside. So, in other words, whatever we want to create, we first create it inside and it will show up in our life. Our life will therefore be the way we see things. Our perception is the key.

Once we've stopped letting ourselves get sick over what we used to perceive as "negative" occurrences, the next step will come naturally. Again, we need find that quiet time alone and calmly tap into our higher self – into the frequency of universal truth that is part of our being. We have to listen to what the universe is telling us and reflect. When we do this, we'll be equipped to course-correct circumstances with our emotions and feelings – the most powerful tools we possess. The universe will hear us, and with just a little action on our part and a lot of universal persuasion, we'll achieve our desires.

After doing this for a while, we'll be able to identify people who only live life in their minds and concentrate exclusively on what's going on outside their souls. We'll feel badly for them and empathize because they really don't know what they're feeling. We'll also be acutely aware of the fact that they're missing out on the joys of life. Plus, no matter how hard they try to change things, we'll observe how they mostly fail because they're acting out instead of feeling within. We'll know that they're disconnected because they refuse to experience the waves of Dualism and let life happen the way it will. There will be a sharp contrast between the way they live their lives, and how we now live ours – successfully with consciousness and a deeper understanding.

* * *

When we change our focus and start living from within, we'll stay centered all of the time. As life happens in all of its intensity, excitements, challenges, struggles, joy, pains, love and frustrations, we'll remain deeply connected to ourselves. Inside – where it counts – we'll stay calm because we'll be totally aware that all is in order and that we are here to experience both sides. We'll see that we designed our life and we are therefore protected. We are more than we think; we just forgot it, but now we'll recognize it once again. While all of this is happening, we'll find the deeper truth of all that exists and be able to create our life with the experiences we want to. But only when we've made peace with both sides of the experiences we came to live through, and are actually *experiencing* them.

We'll start to notice a change in how we perceive everything in our life. A wonderful way to reconnect with our inner world right now would be to sit down and look into the eyes of our child, partner or pet. We don't need to talk or think, just feel. This simple exercise will be intense, touching our heart profoundly and triggering something in our body, as well. We've all experienced moments like this before, perhaps during our very first kiss, or maybe when reconciling with someone we love after an argument. Moments like these feel as though the world is standing still. That's because they are at the core and purpose of our life. They come from deep within. In these moments, life comes very close to us. That's when we feel the deep magic of our existence.

To experience more of these kinds of feelings, all we need to do is to step inside ourselves and stop judging. All struggles, worries, tension and arguments will just melt away. We'll begin to view even the simplest things in life in a whole new way. When we have a discussion with someone and what we're saying is truly united to what we're feeling inside, we'll feel a deeper connection to that person and it will touch our heart. Even when we're arguing with someone, we'll become inspired with a revelation. Maybe that person was missing us and just trying to get our attention by starting an argument. We'll discover the truth of what's really going in between the words. Our deeper truth and understanding will open up to us.

* * *

It is so important to set goals. We need to view having goals as setting an intention. If we don't, then we're just wandering through life with no destination and no plan. For some, goals of wealth and success are first priority. For others, they are partnership and a happy homelife. For most, the goal is a combination of both – the whole pie. We need to be sure to set our goals, but we must also keep in mind that as awesome as they may be, they'll be without meaning if they don't reflect our personal truth. We must do the groundwork (alone time) to find the right path to our personal goals because we are all on our unique journey. Our life actually happens inside ourselves. Therein lies the message, the treasure. Our experiences are gifts – each and every one of them.

Why do so many people find this difficult to achieve? It's because fear is at the core of stopping these folks from connecting to themselves. They only walk on the periphery of life in order – so they think – to avoid feeling anxiety and to build walls of security around themselves. This just doesn't work. Security is an illusion. Real security can only come from the deep understanding of our true divine being.

Think about deep sea divers. The surface of the ocean can be a scary place, especially when a storm is building and cold, gray waves grow violent. However, these divers know that their goal is experiencing the joy, energy and magic that lie in the deep of that ocean, below the surface. They just need to brave the waves and plunge down where everything suddenly becomes peaceful and silent. The deeper they dive, the more beautiful and serene it becomes.

The same goes with life and fear. The outside world is just like the surface of the ocean. If we only focus on it, we'll become frightened and begin to frantically search for safety instead of leaping into our deepest selves, where we'll find our truth. We won't accept the Dualism of both the surface and our inner depth, and that will be a mistake. However, when we plunge deep within our soul and step into our inside world – like the divers descending into deeper waters – we'll find the peace and the truth we'll need to create the life for which we came. We'll totally forget how frightening the surface seemed and know that we're safe. Indeed, there is something magic within.

So, when we stop trying to hold on to imaginary security and allow life to unfold itself, our enlightenment will bring us to the realization that we're here on earth to experience, not just survive. We'll embrace both power and powerlessness, connectedness and loneliness, etc. They come in pairs, and that's our personal life plan, the one we've chosen and created. Then and only then will we become whole and fulfilled.

* * *

The ultimate goal for us all is that we'll no longer be scared to feel. Again, our society can make that a challenge at times. We live with digital information every day. It helps us to do our work and keep in touch with others. However, if we immerse ourselves too deeply into a digital existence, we might be deceived into believing we're actually feeling with our body when in fact we're only experiencing in our mind.

For instance, we might start thinking that we don't need to visit a particular country because we can view it from our computer screen. Or we don't need to learn another language because there's always an online translation tool at our fingertips. We'll watch recipe videos and think our appetite is satiated. Perhaps these things are good for research, but if we don't actually visit that country, learn that language or prepare and eat that dish, we're not living the life for which we were incarnated. We must physically do these things to actually feel them. It all ties into our resistance to connecting with our emotions because of our fear of actually feeling them.

The point is, life is happening to our body. Our emotions help us to experience that life. Emotions and body are deeply connected. We should never fear feeling the ups and downs because Dualism is one of the foundations of life. We can achieve that when we connect to our higher being and stop judging.

STOP ANALYZING, START LIVING

WE WERE ALL TAUGHT AT A VERY early age that 1 + 1 = 2. In practical math, this is true so we should all use this formula when adding up our monthly expenses. The problem is that we all carried this practical way of thinking – namely, logic – into how we view life. When we did that, we learned to live in our minds, analyzing everything for what it seemed to be on the surface and looking for logical reasons as to why it existed. That's not living, because in analyzing with our minds we lost the beauty and magic of living with our emotions. Indeed, for some of us even love disappeared, in its truest form.

The fact is, we shouldn't even attempt to decipher life, at least not in a logical manner, for it's a fool's errand. In the scope of universal understanding, 1 + 1 does not equal 2. There's no place for this formula when learning how to discover who we are and what our true journey is. Life is unpredictable, unique, sacred, magical, confusing and all at the same time vibrant, brilliant and joyous. It's indeed a mystery, but one that doesn't need to be analyzed and solved. Life just needs to be lived.

Science uses logic and analytics all of the time. Of course, this is wonderful when it discovers cures to horrible diseases and methods of making crops grow more abundantly. However, when you think about the amazing advancements science has made in the field of fertility, for instance, why is it that some women just never conceive, or when they do, they can't carry to full term? What happened to all the wonders of science here?

The answer is easy when you realize that the couple really have no choice in the matter. A soul decides to incarnate and then chooses its parents. That is to say, it's the choice of the soul to come to earth and make his or her own journey, not the choice of the parents to have a baby. Highly developed fertility techniques have nothing to do with it. When fertilization does occur, it's just a means to carry a soul through its journey. If we try to use science or even just our mind to analyze this, it seems backwards. Again, there's no room for analytics here.

So, everything I stated so far in this chapter is something everyone knew before they were incarnated. So why did they forget? The problem is that so many folks are not connected to themselves. These people really don't know what's going on inside, but that's where all the answers lie. So, they look outside for reasons and explanations, but in vain. They just can't explain life that way because life is a paradox – crazy, mystical and full of conflicts. There's a magic to it, though, and that no one can deny. We just can't define life in practical, analytical terms.

Here's a question that seemingly comes out of left field: How do we react to the fragrance of a rose? It's actually very pertinent to our discussion and is really more of a difficult question than it first appears. When we smell a rose, something touches us deep inside the moment we inhale the aroma. It's a heady experience that may even make us lightheaded for a moment. If we try to analytically explain and evaluate why we react that way to a simple rose, then the moment, fascination and energy will disappear immediately.

As another example, what do we feel the moment we know we're in love? For most of us, it's something like beauty, spirit and vibration. There's a tingling in our body and soul. Again, the moment we ask ourselves why we're in love with this person, love will disappear. There's no logical explanation for any of it. We just love or we don't. If we really want to experience the love, we shouldn't think about it. We should just step inside ourselves and feel it with emotions from the bottom of our heart.

It's the same thing with music. It can only be created from inside human beings and never from their minds. We therefore cannot really hear it with our brain. If we try to analyze it, we'll never truly enjoy the melody. We can only truly experience music from the inside. Our body is the receptor where the notes can be transformed into a melody. That's why we incarnated into our bodies – to be able to experience such beautiful things as music, love, a sunset, a hug, etc. However, we'll never be able to be deeply touched by the music if we don't allow ourselves to literally "feel" the melody. The joy is in how it touches our soul – not our mind.

I also like to use a music analogy to further discuss why we incarnated into our bodies. A musician may be able to read the notes on sheet music, but no one will be able to experience the magic of the music unless the notes are played on an instrument. In life, our body is the instrument where the music of our soul is created. Real life, like musical notes, cannot be understood with our brains. It can only be felt and experienced through our body. We can know everything about water but we will never know how it is to swim in the ocean unless we have jumped into it with our body. It's the same with a kiss, falling in love, or eating a dish. To experience a country, we have to physically go there, smell it, see it and feel it. Otherwise, we won't experience any of the beauty of the country – no matter how many YouTube videos we watch.

The point is, life must be experienced through our bodies and our emotions. The moment we try to use our minds to analyze and understand anything in life, all true understanding disappears. We must feel life to know life.

* * *

There is actually one way to view the magic of life through science. Scientific evidence shows us that everything in the universe is energy. As we said in Chapter 1, even the smallest piece of every substance, namely the atom, is constantly and permanently moving via that energy. By the way, there is no logic to which direction energy flows and why energy can suddenly be in two different places at the same time. It's a nightmare for the science world because its magical, not logical. In any event, if we accept what science tells us about energy, then we'll be able to grasp the fact that everything is influenced by that energy. It's a constant, universal vibration into which we're all tied, including our emotions.

Understanding this fact can be a powerful tool for us, because we can actually create our life by our thoughts and emotions – via our own energy and therefore through our body, which we use to make things happen. Our feelings and emotions are constantly vibrating and attracting people and circumstances to us. When we step into ourselves and connect with our emotions, we can use them to tremendously impact our decisions, actions and ultimate destiny. The problem is that people really don't connect with whom they truly are inside. They try to analyze everything with their brains and that detaches them from life. They live disconnected from their spirit and their true self, which is pure potentiality. This, in fact, is one of the biggest challenges we encounter in personal relationships because so many people don't understand themselves and therefore cannot relate to their partners either.

John, for example, is a pilot and has made a successful career for himself. In fact, he's so respected that he's only given the longest flights in his airline. It's not surprising that John is so successful as a pilot. Since he was a child he was interested in airplanes. He also had a natural aptitude for mechanics, measurements and calculating everything precisely. He was made for the job.

As for John's personal life, he's been married to Annabel for 10 years. Originally from France, she's quite different than John. Her life centers around passion, positivity and spontaneity. Not a very likely match, and indeed, none of their family and friends could ever figure out why these two extremely different people fell in love and married in the first place. Did John love her for her beauty and spontaneity? Was Annabel attracted to him because of his stability, which would afford her a nice standard of living? Was it a case of opposites attracting?

Well, it seems that both John and Annabel didn't put much soul searching into why they were together. This isn't surprising for John, since he's so analytical and only assesses things – including his personal relationships – with his mind. After 10 years, though, Annabel had enough and was no longer happy in the relationship. So, upon John's arrival from a long trip, she told him, "John, I don't want this anymore. After every trip you come home exhausted and don't want to do anything. You don't even want to talk! I want to live and truly experience life. I'm not getting any younger, John. I want a divorce."

One could imagine, given his personality, how shocked John was. He just didn't get what was going on. Yes, she had told him a few times that she wanted more out of their relationship, but he thought it was just a passing phase. If he advanced his career, he thought, he could afford to buy her more and that would satisfy her. Maybe that was logical thinking to him, but it didn't address Annabel's emotional needs.

"Annabel, I don't understand," he exclaimed. "We have such a nice life together. I gave you a beautiful home and a great lifestyle. It doesn't make sense that you're not happy!" Annabel got angry with his remark. "Those are all material things," she yelled. "You don't understand me at all. You're almost never here and when you are, you're somewhere in your head. I want passion, love and fun. I want to go out, dance and see operas. You don't even like to celebrate New Year's Eve with a party."

Well, John never really got it and the marriage did end in divorce. If John had taken the time to step inside himself and open up to his feelings instead of analyzing with his brain, then maybe he could have related to Annabel on a different level and learned the way to live life. Annabel understood this because she *experienced* life. John, on the other hand, only *existed* and what's more, was trapped in his mind, never allowing life to unfold its magic. Again, we see that we live through our emotions, not through our mind. We can never truly experience life by being logical and organized. Annabel wanted to feel, live and love. John was just focused on the logical side and didn't get that life needs to be lived and experienced.

* * *

The take-away of this chapter so far is that when we try to analyze life and put it all into a logical box of explanations, we destroy it. For instance, when we feel very close to someone or are watching a beautiful sunset, we should just feel how it touches our heart. After doing so for a few minutes, we should then try analyzing why. The moment we do that, our beautiful emotions will disappear immediately.

It's really simple, but so many find it difficult to understand that life comes to us through our feelings. When we want to deeply experience life – when we want to engage with our true existence – we absolutely must leave our mind behind and start connecting with our feelings. We're not saying that emotions are always easy. Some are indeed painful. Nevertheless, they are all mirrors of our souls and we must accept and embrace them to truly be involved with what's going on inside. That's the only way we'll be able to successfully deal with what's happening on the outside.

We incarnated to create experiences here on earth and therefore must walk through circumstances in the outside world. What will determine our success will be our awareness and the only way to be totally aware is to leave analytical thinking behind. Feeling our way through it all is the secret of life.

Practice makes perfect, so we all can start by stepping into ourselves today. After a while, we'll begin to view life differently. When we learn to engage this world through our emotions, perhaps we'll be able to help others do the same. They'll understand, as we do, that without feelings there is no meaning, no passion, no vibrance and no life. Embracing everything life has to offer is why we are here.

Some Things to Think About...

We've already talked about how to meditate in order to step inside and observe yourself. The next step is to learn how to stay in your center and keep connected to your feelings in every situation throughout your entire day.

Try observing yourself in your outside environment. Life will sometimes be vibrant and happy and at other times challenging and intense. Just keep breathing and stay in your center by focusing on your inside. Allow everything to happen on the outside without judging it or trying to change it. Also, don't change your inside feelings to reflect what's happening outside. That will only make you hyper-active or worried. Just feel and observe those inside feelings and what is happening deep within you and remain consistent.

It's important to note that you can change what's happening on the outside if you want to. Don't be detached from your surroundings. However, you must always accept all of your inside emotions without trying to alter them. This will set you free and release your tensions.

In the beginning, you might become distracted and fall into your old pattern of avoiding your emotions. It happens to all of us because it's just a habit. However, the more you practice, the more you'll notice another level of being open up for you.

Keep at it and after some time, it will be easier for you to stay centered. That's when an inner shift will occur. You'll deeply understand that no matter what, you're safe. You'll also start to feel the bigger picture of your journey and instinctively know that you have the power within you to create your life. The waves of life's dualism will become second nature to you and they won't throw or frighten you like they did before. You'll see the beauty in both sides and let it all happen just as it should. You'll feel all of it inside yourself. All is fine, all is intense, all makes you feel vibrant and alive.

It's important to note here that although you are consistently focused on your inside feelings, you incarnated in order to act and create in the outside world. You therefore must participate in everything life has to offer. Go ahead and fight, pursue power, discuss, love, jump into the ocean, cry, dance, scream. BUT while you're doing it all, remain connected to your feelings and your true self. NEVER avoid or ignore your feelings – even those of fear, tension, sadness or loss. Don't try to suppress or manipulate your feelings by popping a pill or putting on loud music or calling someone. That is not being present in life and will only lead you to feel empty. Your soul came all the way here to know what how everything feels, including fear and sadness.

Keep practicing and you'll discover a deeper understanding of the immensity of your soul and your journey. That's when you'll be able to live your life fully. You'll become fully aware that you're safe and never in danger. You're here for a purpose and you're protected.

Remember, your soul is your director, your life is the stage and you are the actor. Enjoy your role – the one you chose for yourself.

AT THE CORE...
YOUR EMOTIONS

WHEN PEOPLE HAVE A WISH OR DESIRE, what they're really longing to experience is a feeling or emotion. It's true, when we want to achieve or attain something in this material world, what we're really searching for is not material at all. It's emotional.

Our fears and desires are based on the very same structure. They're identical – energy-wise – and very much like two sides of the same coin. The interesting thing is that whether we're talking about fear or desire, it really all boils down to emotions. Desires are something we definitely enjoy experiencing. As for fears, we look to avoid them. However, we see that they are exactly the same the moment we understand the emotions behind them. That's when we have the opportunity to break through and by doing so, tap into our power to create our lives instead of being victims of circumstances.

It would be helpful at this point to take a look at how fear is closely connected with our emotions and understand that mechanism. We'll find that fears and the pressure that arises from them appear mainly in relationships, or in situations where we need to deal with other people. Most of us have experienced fear in a relationship and for certain, emotions such as jealousy, guilt, powerlessness or loneliness, are at the core.

To grasp what's really happening in these circumstances, let's examine a couple of situations and then talk about how we can set ourselves free from fear. In our first scenario, we have two friends, John and Thomas. They've known each other for a very long time and it has indeed been a great friendship. John is the more successful of the two, while Thomas has been less of an achiever. Therefore, one of the dynamics of their relationship is Thomas' admiration of John. So, this has not been an equal partnership in the truest sense of the term. John has always been more of the boss – the strong one – and has dictated most of what they do together. John, on the other hand, is shyer and passive – the follower in the relationship. He possesses a lack of self-confidence, mostly because he's not a big money-earner.

One day, John and Thomas meet for dinner. (Of course, John chooses the restaurant.) When they get into a discussion about politics, it becomes apparent that Thomas has changed his views, given the political climate, and no longer agrees with John. To John's surprise, Thomas is actually passionate about his viewpoints and when John tries to sway him to his side – as he normally does – Thomas digs his heels in, holds his ground and defends his beliefs. This is the first time John and Thomas aren't on the same page.

Of course, Thomas is shocked. He becomes very upset and even angry that his friend, who is always so "agreeable," is now behaving like a "rebel." Is Thomas overreacting? Well, perhaps, but what might he truly be feeling? Which emotion is fueling his anger? I would venture to say that Thomas might be feeling powerless at this moment. All of these years he's been the "big guy" in the relationship. He had all the answers and dictated the conditions of the friendship in terms of what they would do together and even what they would discuss. Now he suddenly feels "small" and what's more, somewhat powerless because he doesn't have a strong impact on Thomas anymore. He also feels that Thomas no longer respects him the way he used to.

Or perhaps the emotion of loneliness is at the core of John's anger. He might feel that the end of his friendship with John is near. He might even feel guilty – either consciously or subconsciously. After all, he's dominated Thomas for such a long time and very rarely supported him as an independent person with views of his own. John might even be feeling inferior. Perhaps he always did, but tried to offset this emotion by overpowering Thomas to prove he was superior. However, now that he can't be the boss of John any longer, his suppressed lack of confidence is rising to the surface. The anger he is feeling is just a way of avoiding deeper feelings such as guilt, loneliness, etc.

Any one or a combination of these inner emotions might be at the core of John's reaction – or overreaction – to Thomas' sudden burst of independence. The outside manifestation, as we saw, is anger. The shame of it is that he really has no clue as to what's going on inside himself. His awareness stops, as it does with so many people, and anger appears to be the primary emotion when there's so much more going on deep within.

Let's have a look at the root cause of pressure and fears in another example. Marion and George have been married for 20 years and have two teenage sons. One could describe the atmosphere of their home as quite intense at the moment. The teenagers have become challenging, often acting out as kids do at their age. Of course, it's very exhausting for Marion and George and it has put a strain on their marriage.

One evening, George announces that he's joined a public speaking club which will meet every Tuesday evening. Even though she doesn't know why, Marion is somewhat uncomfortable with the idea. Nevertheless, she tells him that she's happy he's found something he likes.

In the coming weeks, George grows to love his club meetings. He makes lots of new friends and even becomes heavily involved in club duties, which includes creating the weekly newsletter. Marion grows more and more worried about John's newfound interests. She even wonders if he's met another woman at the meetings.

So, one Tuesday night Marion explodes and starts a tremendous fight with George. She tells him that he's spending too much time away from her and the family and she wants it to stop immediately. To her surprise, George tells her she's overreacting and goes to the meeting despite her objections.

After such an aggressive fight, Marion finds herself angrier and more jealous than before. Of course, what's really going on is that there are some deep emotions at the core of her behavior. Perhaps she's feeling lonely. After all, she was used to George coming home after work every night, without fail. Now he's out late on Tuesday evenings, and sometimes grabs a drink with a few of his club friends on other occasions, such as debates, etc. Marion isn't used to being alone. Perhaps she's afraid that John will leave her and then she'll be lonely forever.

Or Marion might be feeling inferior and not attractive to George anymore. With her job and family, she thinks she may have let herself go. She never even took off that weight she gained after giving birth to her second son. She's thought about going to the gym after work but just feels too tired and keeps putting it off. Now, when she sees her husband becoming more self-confident as his public speaking improves, she worries that he'll attract other women and leave her behind. This is only compounded by John when he tells her about what great speakers there are in his club – some of them women. Now Marion really suffers from a lack of self-confidence.

Actually, there might be another emotion that's causing Marion's fear and pressure – guilt. Instead of a lack of confidence, Marion might feel guilty that she's let herself go. She's let George down, so to speak, by not taking care of her appearance and not finding new interests together in order to improve the marriage. She can't even control her own children. "Now the whole family is falling apart," she thinks. "What kind of wife am I anyway? No wonder George is moving on.

Another emotion that might be plaguing Marion is powerlessness. She sees George following his interests, making new friends and in effect, reinventing himself. She feels there's nothing she can do about it. Feeling a lack of power might also be there. This is just not how she expected her life to be. She truly wanted to have a good marriage and grow old with her husband. He was and still is the love of her life, but she feels lost in their marriage.

The two stories of John and Marion probably strike a chord for most of us because we've all experienced something similar in lives. It's important to realize that although one of stories is about a friendship and the other a marriage, the emotions behind both individuals' behaviors are similar if not completely identical. It's important to note that sadness, anger or fear are always the "trigger emotions." The emotions that *really* want to come to light, get healed and be transformed are the ones we mentioned in Chapter 2:

Powerlessness
Helplessness
Guilt
Inferiority
Loneliness
Grief or
Shame

Of all the trigger emotions, fear is the one we should pay particular attention to since it is the most common one, showing us the way to underlying emotions that we don't want to feel. As soon as we accept these hidden emotions, we become free and fear disappears immediately. We then start to embrace both sides – powerlessness and being powerful, loneliness and connectedness, etc. Because of the law of dualism, we cannot experience only one part of an emotion without its polar opposite. When we try to avoid one side, we always end up feeling tension. Every person has 1 or 2 emotions which consistently get triggered his or her whole life. These are the experiences for which the soul came in the first place. As soon the person accepts both sides, the person will become whole.

We can now see that behind the many different situations in our lives lie very similar emotions. There's a universality to it, which makes it easy to recognize how emotions are at the core of every behavior we exhibit. It is also key to understand that most of us are never aware of these emotions. That is the deep secret behind fear and unpleasant feelings. First, we react to a situation with a superficial feeling like anger, worry or jealousy, etc. However, we must become silent and look for the emotions behind these surface feelings. As soon as we accept those underlying emotions, whether they be a lack of self-confidence, helplessness or loneliness etc., our unpleasant trigger emotions will immediately disappear and we'll be free to live. In accepting ourselves, we can be at peace with whom we truly are and what happens in our life. We can finally stop running away and fighting feelings. We'll be free.

* * *

Many emotionally disconnected behaviors are highly regarded in our society. One of them is a constant striving for and ultimate achievement of success. However, the question to ask is why a person is successful. Is he or she using the power of fear to fuel success? I've met many, many successful people – including friends and family – who weren't connected to their emotions at all. In fact, they weren't even aware of them. Many of them were carrying a huge feeling of not being good enough and therefore had a lack of self-confidence. So, instead of accepting themselves with all of their feelings of inferiority, they tried to avoid them by striving to be the best student in high school, graduating with summa cum laude in college and then becoming C-management at a high-powered business firm. With all this, even when they were honest with themselves, they still felt a huge emptiness in their lives. They were disconnected and unfulfilled.

The question to ask ourselves is this: What good is all of this achievement if these folks are still unhappy and not fulfilled in their lives? Not much good at all. If they would only make peace with their hidden inferiority and accept themselves as they are, they wouldn't need to fight unpleasant emotions any longer. They wouldn't have to knock themselves out, always striving to be successful – even to the point of exhaustion or making themselves sick. If they were at peace with their lack of self-confidence, they'd be able to think clearly and discover what they'd really like to do in their lives. If, at the end of the day, they realized that they really did want to climb the corporate ladder of success, they'd do it with joy because that's what they love doing. Their motivation would never be trying to avoid the emotion of inferiority. Motive is central here.

At this point, we all need to ask ourselves why we're doing what we're currently doing. If we are afraid of something, we need to step deeper into ourselves to find out which feeling we're trying to avoid. We can never release ourselves from fear and unpleasant feelings if we look outside ourselves. We'd only be using our brain to analyze the situation, and as we saw in previous chapters, that doesn't get us anywhere, if not deeper into trouble. No, we can only find the solution to our fear inside ourselves. In doing so we'll accept who we really are and learn to tolerate and make peace with our feelings. Then and only then will we be free to choose what we really want to do in our life. We'll discover a life that's authentic, intense and joyful when we do things because we want to, not because we're afraid.

Everything that's good and joyful in life is all available to us when we step inside ourselves. Just like Dorothy, the Tin Man, the Cowardly Lion and the Scarecrow in the Wizard of Oz, it was always with us, even when we were searching elsewhere. We just need to look inside for our power source and our answers. Life is happening through our inside feelings. It's just like the diver who finds the surface of the ocean dangerous and rough. When he dives beneath the surface, he finds everything to be quieter and peaceful. Just like him, when we dive through fear and our unpleasant feelings, to the real feelings of our inner selves, we discover a totally new world.

* * *

If we wanted to summarize this chapter in one sentence, it would be this: Self-acceptance and allowing our feelings to just be is the key to true happiness. We should all take the journey and discover who we really are and then learn to accept all of it. We should never be ashamed of our feelings. There's never any need to hide them because they are always appropriate and acceptable. Likewise, we should never, ever avoid our feelings. That will only limit us and our experiences because life touches us through our feelings. We are the diver, and life is always the surface of the ocean – wild, challenging, irritating and confusing. But underneath, deeper, it is fulfilling and joyful. Whatever is happening on life's surface, we should dive into our feelings, discover our real meaning, and find peace.

To be clear, I'm not saying that if we jump on every feeling that arises in us, we'll become happy. What I'm saying is that life happens and connects with us through our feelings. Even if the emotion we discover inside is not a happy one, we'll be able to accept and tolerate it, and even welcome it. We're like a mountainous island in the ocean, with waves of emotions coming and going constantly. Some will be happy and joyous; some will be angry and lonely. We should feel and welcome all of them, without judging, and they won't push and pull us around the way they used to. We just need to remain centered in ourselves. When we accept our life and ourselves just as we are, the emptiness inside will disappear and life can then touch us with all of its intensity. It's important to remember that waves come in but they go out as well. Nothing good or bad lasts forever.

The moment we accept our emotions, we'll instantly fall in love with ourselves. We'll also have so much more energy and will be stronger, both physically and mentally. We'll be home, whole and connected to ourselves and to all that exists. The fight will end and we'll know that we're GOOD ENOUGH – just the way we are – and that all is IN ORDER. We'll understand the bigger picture of life.

Some things to think about...

The goal of the following exercises is to learn to be free to live your authentic life.

Step 1: Sit somewhere silent and take some deep breathes. Relax.

Step 2: Accept yourself totally. What do you like about yourself? What are your "shadows"? See them, feel them, hug them, accept them.

Step 3: What hurts you? Who hurts you? Whom did you hurt? Feel the pain. How does it feel? Where does it manifest in your body? Let it be – don't try to change it. Accept it and then finally let it go. This is true forgiveness.

Step 4: In the next challenging situation you encounter, "stand" still and just feel. Breath and accept yourself as you are. Everything is okay. Stop fighting the arising feelings which might be uncomfortable for you and just allow yourself to be. Feel life coming to you through your emotions.

Step 5: In your mind, open the door to your life every day. Let in all the feelings, even the ones which hit you like a bolt of lightning. Don't try to change or avoid them. When they show up, welcome them and be still. Just observe. Where and how are they manifesting in your body? When you've located them, let them go. Can you already see a pattern? Which feelings are underneath?

Powerlessness
Helplessness
Guilt

> Inferiority
> Loneliness
> Grief or
> Shame?

That night, when you go to bed, reflect on how much "life" you've let come through you that day. You are at peace with everything – with both sides of your feelings and yourself. As you have accepted all of them, you are whole now and at peace with yourself. Embrace that day because it's where you found your true self. You have arrived.

GIVE THAT WHICH YOU WANT FOR YOURSELF

WE'VE SEEN THAT WE DISCOVER AND EXPERIENCE our whole lives through our feelings. We've also spoken about how useful this is in creating experiences and even course-correcting our direction, if we need to. At this point, it's important to remember that we're not here to become better. We are divine souls and possess divine energy. We know everything and we choose our lives precisely, including the characteristics we need to experience what it feels like to forgive, or to have power, or to be free.

This is quite different from what we've been taught. The truth is, trying to improve ourselves and thinking that we need to become better all of the time is utter nonsense. Perhaps we've forgotten our divine nature, but it's nonetheless true. The thing is, deep inside we all know it. When we learn how to effectively meditate in silence, we connect with this wisdom and truth. We are divine.

Since we are here to make our own experiences, we possess great power: the ability to direct our own paths. However, we must keep in mind that everything we do is based on either fear or joy. As we become more and more aware of our feelings, the more clearly we'll see our true motives, i.e. why we're acting a certain way and how that manifests certain results.

Think about why some people go to the gym. It's either because they're afraid of something, such as health issues or body image, or are doing it because they really love to work out and maintain their body. It's usually one or the other. When we become involved in a relationship, it's either because we really and truly enjoy the company of the other person, or we're frightened of being alone. We might even be successful in business, but our motives may surprise us. Perhaps what drives us is the fear of losing security or even living in poverty. Or, we might just love interacting with the business community, delight in the challenge of negotiations and of course, enjoy the financial benefits of success.

These might seem like very simple examples, but they carry a lot of weight. If we act out of fear, we're living in the future or the past. When we act out of joy, we are in the present moment, living in the here and now. Of course, I'm not saying that we shouldn't focus on personal or business success and follow our goals. What I *am* saying is that we should do it because we want to. The entrepreneur who no longer fights his feelings of inferiority suddenly performs his job out of pure joy. He now enjoys building and improving his business or company as he sees it grow and enter more and more markets. The woman who is no longer terrified of being alone can now share herself, her time and her life with someone because she really loves him and not because she needs him. Everything shifts to a totally different energy, motive and intention. Her partner will feel it and never take her for granted.

We all need be more like children in this aspect. When kids play, they enjoy doing it in the moment. They never think about later or tomorrow, or even yesterday. They don't even concern themselves with what benefits they'll receive from playing the game. They go all in and enjoy it for what it is, here and now. As adults, we need to relearn this way of being. When we understand the bigger picture and the direct cause-and-effect relationship between motives and actions, we'll then be empowered to change our motive in every single situation of our life. We'll be free to have huge goals and work on realizing our vision. Even better, we can change our motive and bring our actions to the here and now, enjoying our journey to success every single step of the way, every single day. Then we can say "goodbye" to the tension of hidden feelings such as inferiority and powerlessness because we have now integrated them.

* * *

Let's talk a bit about "giving." When we give a present, the same cause-and-effect relationship between motives and actions applies. We might be giving the present because we enjoy surprising someone and making them happy. Or, perhaps we're doing it to hold onto the person, so they don't leave us to face our loneliness. Offering someone a present is just one of the ways in which we give, and when done for the right motives, giving can be one of the most wonderful ways to connect with our own life. When we give that which we ourselves want to receive, we'll see that the things for which we are searching – indeed, longing – will come to us immediately. Giving what we truly want for ourselves is magical. It changes us and transforms our energy, making us "givers" to a king, instead of being victims, beggars or poor people. Giving what we truly desire makes us wealthy because it wondrously attracts more of what we want for ourselves. It alters our vibrations and makes us feel abundant as a magnet of love, joy, fulfilment, success and wealth. Indeed, it changes our very personality.

When we give what we want, we heal. When we give love, there will immediately be love in our life. If, on the other hand, we want disharmony, then we can start an argument and we will instantly have the discord we desire. The point is, we have the power to create every facet of our lives. It's important to remember, though, that we should never get caught up in being disappointed and sad about the past, because unhappiness will then become our life. We should just give, no matter what's going on, and we'll receive all for which we are longing.

* * *

It's a shame, but people often misuse other people. They step into a relationship because they don't want to be alone. They love the other person, but not unconditionally. There are often hidden motives of which the other person is totally unaware. We see it all the time. A woman might use her partner to gain security or a better status and acceptance in society. Her partner might think there is mutual love at first, but he eventually catches on and sees that she needs him more than she loves him. He's being misused, and in a sense abused, and knows that she will never love him unconditionally. That's sad and so many marriages and partnerships end under these circumstances.

The problem is that so many people don't give what they themselves want in a relationship. They're motivated by other things and indeed, if they weren't battling emotions like fear and insecurity, they would never have been with their partners in the first place. That ends badly for everyone. These people need to stop longing for other people to give them something to relieve their loneliness, inferiority or helplessness. It doesn't work anyway, and is unfair to the person with whom they're in a relationship.

The lesson here is simple. When we accept that we're alone, then we accept our social situation. When we accept and trust ourselves for whom we are and give what we would want for ourselves, namely love, we will not only have love, but we will have it unconditionally. When we accept our partner like he or she is, they will do the same for us.

* * *

So, what are other situations in our life where we can give what we truly want for ourselves?" Well, if we want to have a successful company, we should give our employees what they need to be successful. When we support and motivate them, giving them raises and bonuses, our company will flourish.

When we want to be close to someone, we should give them closeness. This is in many ways the most obvious thing we can do when talking about giving what we want for ourselves. However, it bears repeating: when we're longing for closeness, give it first. We should hug someone, or touch someone, even if it's just on his or her arm. We'll feel closeness immediately, and it's a wonderful sensation. Perhaps we're longing for kindness. Then we should show kindness. By giving what we want for ourselves, everything becomes our own decision. We have the power to get what we want because we're giving what you want. What we give, how we react and the way in which we behave will immediately be reflected back into our life. It's actually very simple, but extremely powerful!

Another great benefit to giving what we want is that our seemingly endless searching will indeed suddenly end. We'll shift, deep within, from a beggar to a king or queen. We should all write the following on a piece of paper and pin it on a wall:

When we are lacking something, we will miss it. When we give, we become *the* source and will have great abundance.

* * *

In closing this chapter, we should all remember that we are not here just to survive. We are here, as we've said time and time again, to make our own experiences. This is much deeper than it seems at first. The truth is, we're here for a grand purpose, and we're protected. Something bigger than us always has our back and it guides us to the path we have chosen in this life. When we become a giving person, we accept the deeper truth of our being. We understand the bigger picture and the awesome power of our soul.

We should also remember that our wishes and desires are not something that we lack, because we already have and own them. Truly, it is through our wishes and desires that we are guided directly to them, as well as our truth. When we give what we want to receive, we then receive.

Some things to think about...

As always, find a quiet place and take a deep breath. Then, step over your ego and ask yourself these questions...

- If I were financially secure and healthy, what would I change in my life? Make a list.

- What am I really longing for? Which emotion is it? Write it down.

- What would truly fulfil me? Jot is down.

- Why do I think I came into this life? Record your thoughts.

THE IMPORTANCE OF SELF-DEFINITION

WE ALL FIND IT DIFFICULT TO MAKE decisions at times. How many times have we thought, "I really should RSVP '*Will Attend*' to this invitation, but I'd rather spend a Saturday night with my family"? What about a boss' request to join her and the office group for dinner? How often do we wrestle with being too tired to attend, yet frightened if we decline it might hurt our job? This kind of indecision often results in our feeling pushed and pulled around in all directions. That, in turn, often causes us to be lost in even further indecision. What we really should be asking ourselves is: "What about me? What about my needs? Does anyone really care about me?"

It's time to realize that we ourselves are the only ones who ultimately care about our needs and are 100% responsible for ourselves. It's therefore crucial to define who we really are and, in exploring ourselves, we'll discover a fascinating journey. Many of us want to be someone or something else – taller, thinner, stronger, richer, prettier, etc. However, we must remember that we created ourselves with the unique ability to make experiences which are important to us alone. Therefore, for proper self-definition, it's so imperative to discover what is most important to us alone. That's when we'll start speaking up for ourselves and sticking to our values.

One of the ways we can define ourselves is by examining our core values. For some, it's family first with their career following second and health in last place. That means they would risk their health for their family and their job. But is that how they really want to live? Does that truly fulfil them? Do they list their values this way out of love, or rather because they're afraid they'll be viewed as a "bad" person if they take care of themselves first?

Maybe others see themselves as career-driven persons, with everything else coming in at second, third and fourth place. Or, perhaps God and spirituality are at the top of their list of values. If a person is having a tough time defining what's most important to him, priority-wise, then he really needs to examine himself more closely and decide exactly what his core values are. It takes some effort and time because we're so used to our habits and old ways of thinking. We also often view ourselves in the image other people paint of us. These obstacles can therefore be so strongly imbedded in our minds that we become totally unaware of what is truly significant to us.

Sometimes it takes an accident, an illness or a divorce to kick start our examination of our true values in order to better define ourselves. When we do so, we'll learn that only we ourselves can discover what's important to us and furthermore, what truly makes us happy. That's when we'll live to stand up for ourselves and that, in turn, will make us "complete" persons. We will feel whole and arrive in ourselves, knowing and understanding who we really are.

I recommend making a top 3 priority in order to decide the bests way for us in any situation. Let's say it's family first, health second, career last. Then when our boss, for instance, asks us to stay longer but our child has a theater performance, we can say, "I would love to but this evening I cannot. What about tomorrow?" Our boss will have respect for us because we are a person with values and know who we truly are. That builds personality – the personality we have chosen for us.

* * *

Creating an accurate self-definition is not about how, who or what we *think* we should be, but more about discovering what truly and accurately describes us. If we try to remember our energy/vibe when we were children, that would be a good place to start. Then we should think about how we've been as the years passed. Have we been wild and unstoppable? Were we always confident that we could change the world? Or have we been quieter and more introspective? That would mean we've always been more interested in reading, story-telling, daydreaming, fantasy and poetry. Are we still the same today?

We all know something about the science of DNA and genetics, but I believe there is something very much like a "Soul DNA." It remains consistent and it might even take a lifetime for us to discover ours, but it's well worth it especially when we're striving for better self-definition. Each and every one every one of us is truly one-of-a-kind and the entire universe would be so much different without us. Our soul made this journey with predetermined relationships and agreements with other souls in order to fulfil our purpose. We therefore must remain true to whom we really are, because anything else will make us sick – spiritually, emotionally and even physically. We need to take the time to self-define and we'll discover that there is really something very special about each one of us. To ascertain exactly what that is, it's important to understand everything about ourselves, especially our fears and the emotions that cause us to be frightened. When we can truly accept all of them and make our peace with them, then we can step into our true being and power, and express that to the world.

* * *

Someone once said, "We are not afraid of what scares us. Instead, we are afraid of our amazingness!" What does that mean? The thing with fear is, once we've accepted it and the feelings behind it, it magically disappears. We're then free to live and be who we really are. Therefore, in learning to define ourselves, it is also helpful to recognize what our fears are because that is very much a part of whom we are.

Here's a great example that illustrates my point. Elizabeth is a woman who always defined herself as shy. She went to a life coach to get rid of that feeling of being self-conscious and having hot flashes when someone started talking to her, or when she got any kind of direct attention from other people. When she worked with him on it and did some self-discovering, what she found was that she was actually dressing and styling her hair to be almost "invisible" in a crowd. Why? To protect herself from men and other people from seeing her as an attractive, vibrant woman. So, Elizabeth was incorrect in defining herself as shy. She was scared. Scared of what? You see, deep down she was really frightened of closeness. Having men and friends being attracted to her could only make them want to be close to her and she was subconsciously terrified of that.

So, her coach asked her to buy some new, more attractive clothing, get a new hairstyle and start using makeup. She was reluctant at first, but the coach asked her to work with him, and she did. The next time she met with her coach, she told him how intense and scary it was when men looked at her flirtatiously, opened the door for her and even asked her for a date. She said she at times wished she could be "invisible" again, but couldn't help feeling exuberant. "It was so intense and exciting," she explained. "It was like I was kicked out of my own shoes! It felt as if I were flying. What a feeling! I love my new me."

So you see, Elizabeth needed to accept her fear of closeness and embrace herself – showing the world who she really was. Then and only then would she be able to truly know and enjoy how it feels to be attractive and experience closeness and intimacy. Yes, it's what frightened her most, but it's also what fulfilled her the most. The point is, our fears always show us the way to our life's purpose and therefore help us in defining who we really are.

Today, more and more people are becoming awakened and are asking themselves and others questions like: "What is life really all about and is there a deeper meaning than is apparent on the surface?" Even CEO-level executives are pondering these questions in order to better define themselves and become more successful business people – and human beings. As the problem of mental illness is increasing, we're at a point in our evolution where we need to change our focus on the outside world to becoming more aware of who we are on the inside as a means of more precise self-definition. We have to reconnect to ourselves. After all, that's where our true reality and life lie. And whatever we want to create in the outside world always starts solely from inside ourselves. There is where we find our life source. Only a fulfilled life is a life truly worth living – a healthy way of being.

* * *

When I talk about being aware, I'm really referring to creating and understanding our self- definition so that we're clear (aware) about what our values are and who we truly are. That gives us a chance to fill the gap that exists when we want to be someone else. Thinking about who we are and how we want to express ourselves will absolutely empower us in every facet of our life. Truly, to discover who we really are is much more intense, huger and more exciting than anyone could ever imagine. It's the doorway to living fully, authentically and intensely. It's the end of being lost. We will finally arrive. It's the first step to being in our true power and being, and that includes being at peace with the emotions behind our fears. That, in and of itself, is a formidable tool – and gift – from the universe.

Some things to think about...

- Think about what is really important to you. Write it down and structure it in a way that you have "fields" or "areas" as headers. For example, "Family," which represents your partner, children and relatives. "Health," which consists of your diet and fitness lifestyle. "Spirituality," which comprises your meditation practice, faith and time to listen to podcasts or even reading a book that helps you to be in touch with inside reflections. Or "Career," which includes things besides your job or business, such as workshops, social media presence, networking, etc. Then make a list in form of a sequence and decide what's in first, second and third place. Whenever you have to choose between one of these in any given situation, you'll immediately know which one is more important to you and give it priority.

- Think about how you were as a child. Maybe you'll be able to recall what you wanted to become when you grew older. What was your energy like? How was your temper? Reconnect to your little, inner child and integrate that aspect of yourself once again with your awareness as an adult. Feel the emotion of completion.

- Write down a list of who you are *now*. How would you describe yourself to a stranger? Which name would you give yourself? Who are you really? A healer, a warrior, a teacher, a philosopher? Are you stronger than you allow yourself to show? Then get ready to be as strong as you really are. Or are you more sensitive than you allow yourself to show to the world. Then talk openly about your sensitivity and allow yourself to freely express that. Get ready to become who you really are. You are unique and the world is waiting for what you have to share!

10

THE ILLUSION OF SECURITY

DESIRES AND FEARS HAVE THE SAME STRUCTURE. They're just the opposites of each other. We've already talked about what's behind what we *think* we want, but it bears further discussion. We've all desired a certain item, a house, an award or more money from our job at one time or another. But the truth is, what we're really searching for is a particular emotion. For example, when we want to buy an expensive watch or car or even handbag, what we're really desiring just may be to experience the self-confidence we feel when other people see us with these luxury items. They look at us and are impressed, and that feeds our inner need. When we want to own a house, it's most likely the feeling of security that we're desiring, instead of the material house. An award would also give us self-confidence and respect, and earning more money would afford us the feeling of being powerful and having security. Therefore, it's not the actual award or raise in salary that we truly desire; it's the emotions – which they raise in us – that they satiate.

So, these inner emotions that we wish to feed with material things in the "outside world" are what we need to address. I find that the emotion that takes front and center is very often wanting to feel secure and safe from danger, either with a partner or lots of money, or both. It's important to remember, though, that nothing is really secure in life and moreover, it doesn't need to be. Actually, when we open up to the unknown instead of clinging to security, unlimited opportunities will show up and we will step into our pure potentiality to create whatever we desire. Our souls know our particular journey and incarnated to create wonderful experiences on this voyage of ours.

Therefore, when we keep in mind that we're not really in danger, that we're always secure, and that security is in reality an illusion anyway, we'll be ahead of the curve. We won't search for things to help us feel secure because we'll know we are indeed safe and are able to create whatever we want from inside ourselves – from our thoughts and emotions. The funny thing is, people who earn more money and accumulate lots of material things usually feel more and more insecure with every acquisition. They are also so obsessed with losing it all. They lost their connection to their inner divinity and are totally dependent on the material things outside. On the other hand, people who make the effort and discovered their true potentiality and are connected to their own divine source always create what they need, effortlessly and without limits. They are never afraid to lose their wealth, because they know they carry the possibility of creating abundance inside themselves. They know, deep inside themselves, that they are always secure. They are free to be an unlimited creator again and again.

We'll come to realize that real secureness only exists inside ourselves when we're finally aware that we're so much more than we thought we were. Yes, we're conscious in the here and now, but we're only in this life in its particular form for a period of time. Our consciousness is grander than we think. We always were and always will be. Given that knowledge, I find it best to concentrate on what we really want to experience in our life *now*. Which feelings do we want to feel? For what are we deeply longing? We should write it down and get some clarity around it. We should also push the expectations of our family and society far away from us and accept our fears. That's when we'll discover what our deepest "soul desires" are. That will give us real peace and a higher understanding of our life's purpose. That's when we can start setting up our goals – OUR STARTING POINT!

* * *

To begin setting some goals for ourselves, we first need to define our most profound desires. What are they?

- To become a CEO?
- To live in a foreign country?
- To become an artist and gain fame?
- To live on a farm or on top of a mountain?
- To become a monk or a pilot?

Ask yourself, "What would I do if I had $100,000,000 USD in my bank account and were financially independent? What would I do if I could afford everything I wanted?"

When we truly discover what our real desire and goals are for this particular journey in this specific lifetime of ours, we should then start digging deep down to reveal the emotions behind our desires, the ones we want to feel. We need to identify them and become intimate with them. We should try to imagine how we would feel the moment we achieved our desire. What would it be like doing what we really like to do? Where in our body would we feel it? This is really important because it will increase our vibration and speed up the universal process of attraction. It will all come directly to us because we've connected with the universal mind and power through our feelings and vibrations. That's the secret!

* * *

At times, many of us wonder how we can achieve a more joyful energy and vibration when we're always worrying about finances, health or relationship problems. How can we get to this higher ground when we feel so depressed and discouraged? The answer is rather simple: We need to give the negativity away by handing it to the universe. When we do that, we'll shake off the undesirable emotions immediately. We should grab a tea or coffee, take a deep breath and concentrate on what we really want. Order ourselves to "Stop!" when our mind begins to tell us that we should be complaining and worrying. Ignore those intrusive thoughts, even if we need to listen to some soulful music or repeat affirmations. Or dancing to your favorite music by yourself to drive out the negativity is also a great option.

When we've accomplished this and begin to truly and closely know the emotion that will rise in our body when we've achieved a goal and are living the life we want to, then we can empower that particular emotion to achieve that goal. Perhaps it's a feeling of self-confidence, power or value that arises when people we respect recognize us for the amazing persons we are. We should step into that emotion. Dress the part and carry ourselves with a powerful and erect posture. Sit upright, breathe deeply, smile and send ourselves some love and faith. That's when the vibration changes for us. Even the small things in our life will make such a huge difference. We just need to step energetically into that new "us."

The universe brings us exactly what we ask for through the emotions we put out there. So, we must pull ourselves out of any doubtful, negative emotions. Just like changing our coat, smile, be confident and carry ourselves like a person who is where he or she wants to be. Then we can set our sight on those goals and watch what happens!

Some things to think about...

At times, do you feel lost and overwhelmed, thinking that your goals seem to be unreachable? If so, you can reconnect to yourself, remembering how commanding you are and that you have it all in the palm in your hand.

Let's try a powerful breathing technique. In stressful situations and on busy, hectic days, we often don't breathe deeply enough. I'm not talking about just breathing into our chests. Breathing into your belly will bring you not only calmness and inner strength, but it also brings you back to your center, helping you to be more focused.

IN THE STORM OF LIFE

You can use this technique anywhere
and at any time of the day:

Sit down and begin to breathe into your belly. Breathe in, breathe out. Slowly in, slowly out. Observe the movement of your belly and calm down. Try it before a difficult discussion with your partner, before an important meeting or presentation, in a doctor's waiting room, anywhere. You'll find that it will help you to prepare for your next move/action and to strengthen yourself. It will reconnect you to your true being.

Useful affirmations:

You might want to try using some powerful mantras to keep your mind focused on your goals and positive outcomes. There are some extremely effective ones out there. You just need to find the one which resonates with you on your emotional level.

> I love the one from the book "The Secret":
> I am whole,
> perfect,
> strong,
> powerful,
> loving,
> harmonious and
> happy.

Or try this one to deeply reconnect to your soul and true being:

> I AM.

11

THE POWER OF THOUGHTS

WE'VE ALL HEARD ABOUT THE POWER OF positive thinking many times. Some of us might think to ourselves, "Oh, that again! I feel terrible but I just don't have the energy to change my negative thoughts right now!" That's normal, and it happens to all of us at one time or another.

In my experience, we're sometimes so intensely influenced by stars, constellations, moon cycles, seasons, news, situations, catastrophes and energy that what we need to shift into a positive direction feels impossible to achieve. It's as if we're pretending to be someone else when in reality we're really not doing well and have to challenge ourselves to stay positive.

What we need to remember, though, is that emotions follow our thoughts and thoughts attract outside circumstances. Therefore, our thoughts are our most important tools when it comes to manifestation. But how can we manifest positive things when we have a negative setback?

As we've discussed, the connection to the universal truth and all solutions, as well as our power source, exists inside ourselves. So, therefore, to change anything, we need to alter what is happening inside ourselves and change that first. Of course, it's easier than it first appears. When we continue to have negative thoughts, we are in a judgmental mode. We *think* we know what's right and what's wrong. Therefore, it makes sense for us to blame someone or something for our problems. BUT the shift happens when we change our focus. That's when we take full responsibility for our life and leave behind what is no longer good or working for us.

Taking this step is crucial. How often do we feel like we're obligated to do something and then are irritated about how it makes us feel? Then, of course, we start to think that we should be feeling differently about it all. Well, we're having all these bad feelings because we really don't like doing certain things in the first place, such as going to a certain event or being in a particular situation or living where we do now. The point is that we cannot change and manifest what we want when we continue to do what doesn't work for us. That's why traveling is so helpful. We see the world "from above" and get distance even from our current energy. When we return home, we see it all in a different perspective and that helps us to know what to do.

When we're ill, for instance, we should focus on healing, get the medicine we need and take care of ourselves. We need to enjoy the love that we're giving ourselves. We shouldn't be angry because we can't do our work or clean the house or prepare dinner. We just need to cancel our appointments and take time for ourselves, to heal. We should do the same thing in every aspect of our life. We must not be so hard on ourselves. Acceptance helps us to heal and is so helpful when we don't get what we want.

When we're with people who always complain, they end up stealing our time, our energy and our joy. We mustn't let them do that to us. Instead, we should focus on things, places, groups or people who are supportive of us. The only way to change our life is to change where we put our precious thoughts. When we make that change and move with baby steps at first, we'll soon see a difference in our life.

* * *

What we've talked about teaches us that when it comes to positive thinking, we don't need to manipulate our true feelings. Instead, we should hug them all – the anger, the frustrations, the sadness, the depression. Then, with the acceptance that things are what they are, we can make that shift and contemplate what we really want. What is the solution we're seeking? What is our dream if we could afford everything and have it all? We must not allow any limitations to hold us back. What is it that we want? BUT we should decide from our heart, not our ego. We need to determine what we really and truly would like to have or do. Then we should think about that and focus on it. We will discover step by step how to get there and then we will only need to take action accordingly. We can hand the details over to the universe. That's when the shift happens and life starts to offer us magical opportunities and unbelievable solutions.

I know, if feels scary and virtually impossible at first. However, when we're aware and observe ourselves, we'll immediately see a difference in our feelings and vibrations. People often ask me how I managed to relocate a few times to different countries around the world. They want to know if I was scared. I tell them that I actually used the same method we're discussing here to make it happen successfully. That's why I know how it works so well.

So, what was my process? Well, it began when I felt stuck, realizing that my life's situation was convenient but not truly fulfilling me. When I felt that life was passing me by, I would ask myself, "What would I do if I were to have $100,000,000 USD in my bank account and didn't have to worry about money at all?" That's when I reconnected with my true self – my spiritual power source – and realized that I wanted to learn something new or live in another country and having a different lifestyle. It's a running theme for me. So, I started to research everything about a certain country or a new business or job. I imagined what I would be doing if I were already in that country or at the new job. When it felt great and exciting, I continued to look into what I needed to make that change. I started to reach out to people, agencies to find a home or visa consultants to ask what I would need for the move. Or if it were a new job or business, I'd research what I needed to learn before going after it. I actually made a proper list of what I needed to do to get where I wanted to be. Secondly, I focused on how.

After just a few days, I was already all in – heart, body and soul. I got so excited because I could actually start to plan and use my capabilities to make that move or job happen. It was always easier than I thought. I learned and was always reminded that limitations are only in our heads. What's more, I also gave my desired wish to the universe, letting it go with trust that it would all happen in the right way and at the right time. Finally, as we'll talk more about in a later chapter, I created a vision board and uploaded it as a wallpaper image on my phone. The vibrational shift already happened and the only thing I had to do was to focus on the move or new job and keep moving.

Of course, I sometimes woke up in the middle of the night and was frightened. But I would get up, take a deep breath and think about what was scaring me. I started to realize that if there were a lack of money, I'd figure out how to get it. Maybe my bank would work with me, or I'd sell something. There was always a way. All I needed to do was to face it and start dealing with what scared me directly. The fear always disappeared and I found not only a solution, but also my strength. That fulfilled me so that I could overcome my obstacles.

It works every time. We just need to be careful not to send mixed messages to the universe. That could make getting what we want really difficult. We need to be crystal clear about what we desire for it to work. Let's say there's a side of us that's longing for a deeply intense relationship, but another side that has us unsure whether or not we're ready to give up our independence. That's when we'd be sending mixed messages out to the universe. Our energy won't be focused and we won't reach our goal.

Every decision requires sacrifices. For whatever it is we want, we have to do something or give up something. That's why we can only be successful when we do the work, dig really deep inside and know what we really love. Going to work will no longer be an effort; we'll love what we're doing and work harder at it. We'll adore giving ourselves to someone because we'll be whole and in the relationship for the right reasons. That's living a joyful life. That's what I want for all of us!

Some things to think about...

We've learned that the way to happiness is to be clear about what you really want. Let's direct your thoughts toward the end goal and get started now. Don't allow any emotions to change your course. Keep your thoughts laser focused on solutions to getting you where you want to be.

It's not your job to need to know how. Just trust that it will happen and the universe will sort the details out for you. That's the job of the universal mind.

Try this exercise to get started:

- Sit silently and imagine you possess all possibilities

- Be honest!

- Ask yourself, "What would I really like to be? Where do I want to be and why? What do I want to do?" Is this wish coming from your heart?

- Start researching everything about it and find out what you need for your change/move, etc. Write it down. Now your wish becomes a goal.

- Focus on the final goal and don't let any doubts or limited believes let you give up on it.

- Set a time frame as to when you want to achieve your goal or be where you want to be.

- Observe your shift

- Keep going and get what you truly want.
  One step after the other. It is possible!

Your thoughts are the rope with which you climb the mountain!

THE ILLUSION OF YOUR COMFORT ZONE

WHAT IS THE SO-CALLED COMFORT ZONE? MOST would define it as a place or situation where we feel safe and in control. That definition is fairly accurate. What's more, we are all born with a natural impulse that triggers us to want to remain in our Comfort Zone. However, we need to ask ourselves this: Are life and work so dangerous that we're always facing death and need that instinct to survive? I would say no, at least not in developed countries where there is no civil war raging all around us. On the one hand, a Comfort Zone is very useful in that it eases anxiety; however, it stops us from achieving self-development and experiencing more in our lives. This in and of itself makes the Comfort Zone a hinderance and something for which we should not be unceasingly searching.

So, what can we do to really step out of our Comfort Zone – to try more, explore more and do more – and yet still feel confident and in control? The thing of it is that we have hundreds of voices in our heads every day – a continuous and permanent inner communication going on that gets in our way. It's like sitting at a table full of delegates from different states – "states of being," that is, or we can say "emotions" as well – all voicing their opinions.

For example, when we're facing a new opportunity, our Fearful Voice might say, "Oh my God, I'm not sure if I can make it through this!" The Adventurous Voice is concurrently telling us, "I cannot wait to do this! I've never tried anything this exciting before!" At the same time, our Cautious Voice warns us, "Let's get all the facts first, and then make a decision." Then our Workaholic Voice quickly states, "Let's first do our job. I'm not sure I'll have any energy left afterwards, so we'll see. Remember, work comes first." Of course, the Tired Voice chimes in, "Must we do that as well?" while the Restless Voices says, "When can we start?"

All of these voices are totally normal. However, if they're all speaking at once, creating emotional turbulence, then how can we find our way and make the right decisions?

Well, first we must realize that all these thoughts and voices are there to tell us to do things in a certain way, help us to have more control over our decision-making and let us be able to step out of our Comfort Zone by taking calculated risks. On the other hand, when our inner voices are saved and fixed in old, unrealistic and out-of-date phrases, they can block us from experiencing more and keep us tight in our Comfort Zone. So, what's the answer here? What we should do is observe which thoughts are coming up and make sure they are ones that will help us to see our new venture from different angles. This will help us to find the right decision on how to explore more. In addition, we should eliminate and delete the thoughts in our head that hold us back for no good reason.

It takes some doing, but when we become aware of all the repeating mantras and beliefs these voices tell us every day, then we can change them to our advantage by using affirmations to help us emerge from our Comfort Zone and discover new possibilities. This is a very old and proven technique that will help us to alter the thinking patterns of our mind. Simply stated, affirmations are positive statements that can help us to stop sabotaging our life with negative thoughts. In effect, simply affirming the positive things that we want to feel will get us to our end goal. They could be emotions, beliefs, values, desired outcomes, etc. Whatever they are, we need to believe and affirm them to be true and present in the moment. The more we repeat these affirmations, the easier behaviors that can sustain our goals will become. At the end of this chapter we'll look at some useful affirmations to help shift our life from negativity to positive thinking and achieve what we truly desire.

* * *

At this point we know that engaging life through our feelings is very, very important; however, there is something bigger. It's our soul – our inner wisdom which is part of the grander universal understanding. This higher consciousness knows all the answers and our journey in its entirety – our life as a whole. As we've discussed, our mind is just simply not capable of doing that. Our soul affords us the opportunity to understand what is truly going on in our life and to become an observer of ourselves. I call it an Active State of

Meditation. With a little bit of inner distance, we'll be able to see and understand the bigger plan of our life's journey and all the connections in between.

We've said it before but it bears repeating: We need to look deep within to connect with our true self. If we don't then we'll be detached from our soul and emotions and we won't be able to see and feel the bigger meaning of everything that's happening in our life. We also might not be able to grow aware of the immensity and power of our soul and all that makes us wonderful. With detachment, we can't see the whole map of our life as we would view the world from way above in a space shuttle. Yes, when we're detached our mind thinks that our life ends at a certain point. However, when we're in touch with our soul we see and understand that nothing ends. On the contrary, everything keeps moving. There is no completion to our life, just changes in the state of appearance of the particular life we're in right now. All our lives follow the same "red line," the same core philosophy. We may be worriers or philosophers. Our soul might be a healer, a reformer, an artist or a leader. Only the scenery changes in our different lives. Our core purpose stays the same.

It's very difficult to comprehend all of this when we haven't created any experiences outside our consciousness, like with hypnosis. As I did it for a whole year, I'd like to share this knowledge: We are always safe and we always have control over our life. It's all totally in our own hands. We choose our journey and have the power to guide our thoughts and create what we want. We therefore can select and change our beliefs. I'm not just using "positive thinking" words here (although they are). I'm speaking of the deep truth about our being.

So, what does all this have to do with our Comfort Zone? Although it's a natural instinct that self-activates in certain situations to make sure we survive, we really can experience so much more than that. We are free, we are protected. Even if our mind cannot see or grasp the whole picture of our entire being, our soul – our inner wisdom – can. That's why meditation always brings us back to our own deep soul source, our own truth.

Remember, we're here for a purpose, not just simply to survive. We need to rise above the limitations in our head and make an affirmative decision to step out of our Comfort Zone today. What we're afraid of will actually fulfill us most!

Some things to think about...

Here is a powerful exercise I'd like you to try:

The next time you're under a great deal of pressure, closely observe the situation and yourself, and then ask:

"What is it I'm really afraid of? Being powerful, carrying responsibility, being free, being in love, being connected, being strong, being hard, being alone, being dependent?

Which emotions would that particular experience or fear rise in you? Are you ready to feel them? Go ahead and give it a try. In the very end you'll understand that you're afraid of being truly happy. That seems to be a paradox, but it's the truth and many philosophers have spoken about it at length. The sensations of experiencing true happiness are so intense that we're frightened to really feel them and therefore sabotage ourselves.

Once you've really understood that you incarnated to create experiences, then your life will change. Your deep fear to survive will disappear and you'll feel that you're free and protected. You'll start to truly live and experience it all.

Let's use some affirmations…

You can employ affirmations to change your beliefs and behavioral patterns. First analyze the thoughts or behaviors that you'd like to change in your own life and career. Then turn them around and come up with positive thoughts and behaviors that you believe will help you reach your desired goals.

People practice affirmations in different ways. You can write them down, say them aloud or repeat them silently often throughout your day. It's crucial to truly believe in them, though, for that's when they become powerful and create manifestations. Here are some examples that you can use. Or create affirmations that feel authentic for you:

- I am strong
- I am successful
- Success is my birthright
- I allow myself to be successful
- I invite money into my life
- I am wealthy
- It is good to be rich
- I love myself
- I am lovable
- I trust myself
- I believe in myself
- I am confident
- I can accomplish anything

Whatever is important to you, you possess the power to change or create your beliefs to support it by repeating your affirmations as often as you can. After a while, your mind will think in a different way and expect different outcomes. In addition, your body will follow your mind. This is in effect a reprogramming of your subconscious.

Step out of your Comfort Zone, see and remind yourself of the total picture of your being and become aware of how powerful you really are!

LET YOUR HIGHER CONSCIOUSNESS TAKE OVER

WE ALL HAVE FOUND OURSELVES IN A situation where we're unable to make a decision and really don't know what to do. Maybe we've experienced a setback and feel empty or lost. Perhaps we were dealing with a real catastrophe, such as the pandemic we all faced with COVID-19. I'm sure you'll agree that these situations are terrible because they make us feel so powerless and helpless. The truth is, the problem almost always stems from losing the higher connection to ourselves and our souls. This loss leads us to also disconnect from our true power.

When we find ourselves in these circumstances, we need to realize that there is a deeper meaning to our being and our life, even if our mind cannot fathom it. What's more, we can truly connect to a higher energy and intelligence for assistance. This support is hidden from us and we're not able to tap into it when we rely solely on our minds. It's beyond our brain's imagination and we've all at times thought, "It's impossible that there's something so big that it can influence and support every single human being on this planet." However, let's look at it another way. What if every single human being on earth is a part of this energy and intelligence – one with it – and each of us is just incarnating into different forms while we're here as human beings. Then it doesn't seem so impossible that the universal energy can influence each one of us because we're all part of it, as one. And that is indeed the case.

This universal energy is intelligence, yes, but it's also vibration. As we discussed, everything around us – in the whole universe – is pulsating and vibrating. Nothing stands still, and we can see that in the fact that all the planets of our solar system are constantly moving. Indeed, everything in the universe is in motion and exists out of vibration, like energy. Since we're all part of this universe, we therefore exist out of this vibration and energy as well. So, when we become aware of our vibration and change or adjust it in every needed situation to our advantage, we have a very powerful tool with which to work.

Let's talk about the vibrations found in sounds. Sound vibrations, when coming into contact with us through our bodies, have an effect on us physically, as well as mentally, emotionally and spiritually. In fact, they can literally alter the patterns of our brainwaves, breathing and even our heartbeats. Science has shown that the origin of perfect vibration is found in the sound of OM, which was originally derived from Hinduism. In fact, many believe that it was the cosmic sound which initiated the creation of the universe and there's actually some scientific fact which may back that theory. When OM is chanted, it vibrates at the frequency of 432 Hz, which is the same vibrational frequency found throughout everything in nature. You therefore can say that OM is the basic natural sound of the universe. Its particular vibration is our pure, flawless energy and being and connects us to nature and all living beings.

There's actually some more science behind the immense spiritual and creative power of OM. Different syllables, when uttered, have different vibration patterns which actually affect different parts of our bodies. The particular sequence of the sounds in OM produce a vibration that can improve our concentration, give us clarity, reduce mental stress and tremendously help us to connect with ourselves. The sound of OM takes us into the deepest state of meditation. It also brings our "Soul Vibration" back to the perfect state in which we were born. We can therefore use the power of OM to immediately release us from depression and anxiety.

Sound vibrations are used as a therapy to promote healing and encourage both physical, spiritual and emotional well-being. In fact, the Tibetan Singing Bowl is a type of metal "bell" that vibrates and produces a deeply beautiful tone that Tibetans have been incorporating into their meditation and rituals since the 12th century. A study conducted in 2016 concluded that Singing Bowl Therapy can help reduce anxiety, depression and fatigue. Therefore, like OM, the Singing Bowl tone (vibration) can help bring us to a better quality of life. This is not a coincidence. A Japanese scientist noticed, quite by accident, that the vibration emitted by Singing Bowls is actually the same as that of OM!

When filling a handmade Tibetan Singing Bowl with water and swinging the wooden stick, we see the water start to bubble. The sound of the bowl is making that happen, and the vibration of that exact tone can have the same positive effect on our physical and emotional state because our bodies consist of 80% water. There's a science to it, so we can use the Singing Bowl to uplift our vibration when needed. That will give us the opportunity to bring it back to the perfect, natural one with which we were born. We'll then be able to eliminate lower vibrational issues such as blockages and illnesses like depression, trauma and anxiety.

* * *

Understanding the information we discussed thus far brings me back to the immense power we all possess – the ability to connect with our vibration to the higher, universal consciousness and power. This is impressive because it then allows us to attract positive circumstances and events and can also constructively influence other people and their vibrations, even if we're not physically with them. Keep in mind, though, that our vibration needs to be consistently high for us to attract and influence in a positive, abundant and successful way. If it's low we'll connect with, attract and encourage negative incidents, losses, illnesses and failure.

Therefore, our vibration is our biggest power source and we can decide how we'd like to keep it – high or low. Of course, we're choosing to keep it high, but how do we achieve that? The answer is amazingly simple: We just need to make a conscious decision to choose where our focus is, where we are to be and with whom we will associate. We should even be meticulous about what we're saying and writing, as well as what information and thoughts we feed our mind. We need to keep it all positive, and use affirmations to manifest achievement of our goals and ultimate success in your life.

It's important to keep in mind that because our higher consciousness is connected to the universal mind, it therefore sees the entire picture of our life and journey – including the experiences and lessons we need to face. When babies are born, they still have that connection for the first few years of their lives. However, they lose it by the time they're about 3 or 4 years old. That's when they start to think of themselves as unique and different entities in the world, and therefore lose the concept of oneness with the entire universe and all the souls in it.

The point is that we need to reconnect with this type of "childlike" understanding to bring us back to the awareness that we are so much more powerful than we could ever have imagined. This delivers us from tricky, stuck and hopeless situations and allows us to be in a position of power – the creators instead of the victims. Of course, we cannot always change what happens in our lives, but we can decide how we react to it. There's always a choice. For every problem there exists a solution; we just have to find it. It's also comforting to know that sometimes even the worst problems bring us something good – more strength, true friends, valuable lessons or new connections.

Another positive side-effect of working with our higher consciousness is that we'll deeply reconnect with our soul and being. This will make us more whole and give us a feeling of completion and connectedness as part of the universe. We'll feel that everything makes sense instead of being overwhelmed by the trials we have to face. Challenges are actually a blessing as they afford us the best chance to grow and enrich our lives.

We must never forget that life is based on dualism. So, if we're facing a huge problem, it's imperative to remember that the opposite is already on its way – victory, release and peace. When the night is at its darkest point, the next day is already starting. We will never be given more than we can carry and never have to face more than we can bear. Our soul has chosen this life and we are safe and guided. So, we should reconnect with the higher consciousness and trust the bigger picture of our journey. The older we get, the more we'll realize the perfection of synchronicity and timing in our life. That in and of itself is power!

Some things to think about...

How do you feel when you're facing challenges in your daily life? It's certainly not a comfortable feeling. When you have a problem and you're running out of ideas on how to solve it – or really don't know how you can manage a certain situation – you can give it all to your higher self and let it solve the problem on another level.

All you have to do is:

- Take 10 minutes out of your day.
- Sit in a quiet space outside or near a window.
- Breath and step into your body, scanning each part of it and being totally aware of your physical presence.

- Then imagine your problem, question or request in a way that you can put it into an imaginary box, like a gift or package.

- Look to the sky and say, "Dear higher self, thank you for your guidance. Today I would like to ask you to [mention your request]. I now give it totally over to you. Please solve it as I step back and let you do your work. Thank you very much."

- Make a real gesture with your hands and give your imaginary box or package to your higher self, reaching your arms out and up to the sky.

- Then let go completely and don't allow yourself to think about it at all! That is very, very important. Do it as if you've giving it to someone you trust – a person you know who will handle it right now and make it a top priority just for you.

- Start doing something totally different.

- Whenever you get a spontaneous idea or an impulse like, "I should buy that book or call that guy," do it! There you will find your solution or direction. There is the next step waiting just for you. The higher consciousness will always solve your problem. You simply must trust the messages you get and take action. Remember, these messages are coming from your intuition, not from your mind, which would only try to analyze the problem and find a solution in an analytical way.

- Trust your higher self…start to move… and soar like an eagle!

VISUALIZATION AS A MANIFESTATION TOOL

*"What you can imagine,
you can achieve,"*
Unknown author

WHEN PLANNING A VACATION, MANY OF US imagine what the resort will look like, or even picture ourselves on the beach sipping a tropical drink. Or before heading into an important meeting, we "rehearse" it in our mind and "see" it as it plays out even before we get there. We all tend to do this at times, but many folks don't realize that there can be great power in it, too. Yes, we can visualize what we want and actually make it happen with what are called Visualization Techniques.

These techniques have been used for ages to aid in the manifestation of desired goals and dreams. In effect, we can visualize in our mind's eye a desired goal as if it has already been achieved to help us actually make it happen. For instance, if we can vibrantly see ourselves living in a big beach house in our mind, we can make it happen. If we can vividly envision ourselves sitting in the CEO's office of our company, we can make that happen, too! It's actually pretty easy to do. We just have to believe what we're seeing as already a done deal – as if it's true now and in the present time. Then FEEL it. The emotions will then attract things and move energy, circumstances and events to manifest our goal.

Many wonder how this can really be. Well, remember when we spoke about positive vibrations attracting positive outcomes? This is very much the same thing. Visualization uses this "Universal Law of Attraction", where same attracts the same, to bring into our life everything we want to rapidly accelerate the achievement of our heart's desires and goals. What we require will be drawn to us in the form of a person, an opportunity, an idea – in person, on a phone call, in a book, through an email, etc. This is because by visualizing we tune our desire into the same frequency on which our goal operates. One thing is for certain, it will come to us and give us what we need to take the proper steps to create our goal and therefore be the master of our own destiny. Is it a super-power? Well, not in the sense of Superman with his X-ray vision, but I do believe we can say that it is. After all, being able to attract what we want by just simply visualizing it in our minds and feeling with our whole body that it is already a reality is a pretty stupendous feat! What's great is that we all possess this super power.

* * *

We've talked about how limited our minds are in terms of capturing the greater picture of our lives. Well, we can actually use that to our advantage when performing Visualization Techniques. Our mind alone cannot really distinguish if what we're visualizing is true or not. It can't "feel" it. (By the way, that's why we so often have problems in making decisions. After all, our mind very often says something vastly different than our emotions.) So, since our mind doesn't really know whether or not what we're visualizing is a reality, we can allow our emotions to take over and believe what we see inside ourselves to be true when we visualize. We'll be able to actually feel it, change our frequency and attract people, circumstances and events which vibrate on the same frequency – the ones we want. Just as different radio frequencies play different music, we attract different things through our frequency as it swings. We should keep in mind to never use our mind to visualize because we want to avoid running into the same old doubts popping up now and then. When they do occur, though, we'll force ourselves with awareness (by decision) to turn those negative "mental" thoughts into positive ones and then continue to focus on our Visualization Techniques as a means achieving our goals.

I recommend doing Visualization every day to be as effective as possible. Just before falling asleep or a few minutes after waking up are often good times for employing these techniques. Of course, it is deep, "inside" work. Life always changes inside ourselves before our inner changes are reflected to the outside world. Think about falling in love. When it happens, we start to feel, speak and walk differently and are so much more uplifted. Our mind cannot guarantee if the other person has the same feelings and whether or not the relationship will work out. Nevertheless, our body feels different emotions, has more energy and puts us in a better mood. This is what the outside world perceives – almost a different person – just because we fell in love on the inside. This inside shift is the target when we use the technique of Visualization.

What's to follow will give you some detailed tips about Visualization. Let's take it step by step so that we can learn to implant it into our daily life and manifest what we're looking to achieve and expect great results!

Some things to think about...

Let's get started on Visualization...

- To begin, it is imperative that you are 100% sure of what you want to attract, because when it arrives it can impact your life, making slight and even bigger changes in your routine. For instance, if you want to become an entrepreneur, you might not be able to enjoy long vacations and you might even need to work on the weekends. If your dream is to travel more, then you probably won't be able to spend as much time with your friends and family at home. Be careful what you wish for!

- Once you are clear about what you truly want, then think about it in a well-defined and vibrant way. Put a detailed image into your head that shows you in the situation or position where you are living your dream or goal. How does that look? What are you wearing, where are you, what time of day is it and who is with you? Most importantly, how do you feel?

- Now, close your eyes and totally "inhale" this feeling or emotional state of being. That's your goal. As I've mentioned before, your body is the instrument where the melody of your life becomes a song to which you can listen. The notes by themselves cannot create the music. An instrument is needed to let the music come to life. Therefore, let your dream become alive by imagining it vibrantly and seeing your goal with your whole body and all your senses. Then let your wish become a reality by feeling that you've already achieved it. For example, when you want to become an entrepreneur, feel like one. Change your attitude and act, speak, move and dress like a business person. See yourself in a great position. When you want to have a relationship, see yourself being committed to someone. Take care of yourself so that you'll feel confident in attracting and being with someone special. If that means that you perhaps need to get into better shape, then go to a gym and pay more attention to your diet, etc.

Do you need some inspiration in finding images to visualize? Here are some ways to look for pictures, photos or images that will trigger emotional responses and help bring your goals to life.

- Start searching the internet. Don't think too much about the actual meaning or sense of the photos or images. Instead, just look at them and observe yourself to see if they resonate with your emotions and make you excited or passionately involved. When you feel the emotional response, then you've located the images you need to become a magnet for your dreams.

- I think it's a great idea to choose one image for each area of your life. For example, one picture of a thousand-dollar bill to represent your desire for financial security, one image with a beautiful home or apartment to reflect how you'd like to live, and another of a romantic, candlelit dinner for your personal life. Or possibly a photo of an airplane that speaks to your longing to travel and an image of a woman at the gym to reflect your desire to be in shape. The possibilities are almost endless. Whatever the image, each one should lift your emotion concerning that area of your life and speak to the goals you want to achieve there.

- Remember, the emotion which the images trigger in you is very important. For example, if you would like to have a job with more freedom so that you can work from wherever you want, you might use an image of a beach, surfboard or a seat on an airplane to achieve that goal. Why? This could evoke the excitement you'd feel at being your own boss and having the liberty to work from places you love to be, instead of an office. For some, a beach can signify a need to vacation more. For you, however, the image of a beach might trigger the feeling of confidence you'll get by being an independent entrepreneur. Take the time to be creative in deciding what images you choose. It will be worth it.

- Once you are clear about what your life should look like and have found images that trigger particularly satisfying emotions in you, print them out. After that, cut them out so that you're holding the photos physically in your hand. If you can, buy a white canvas that you can adhere to a wall and post the photos on it. Or, you can simply place them on a table or floor. Just be sure that you arrange them in a way that resonates with you. For instance, you might want to place the money images on the bottom to signify that your financial needs are secure and are the foundation of your freedom. Then place the more inspiring images, such as travelling photos, closer to the top. You can also place the more basic images on the outside and the image that resonates with your deepest desire right in the middle.

- When you are happily satisfied with your personal vision board, take a photo of it with your phone or camera. This photo is going to serve as your trigger image to shift your focus, concentration, decisions and actions. Then situate it in places where you'll see it often. You can make it the wallpaper on your phone or laptop, or you can print it and hang in in your living room. Where do you spend lots of time? Place your photo there.

Every time you see your vision board, you'll experience an array of emotions. It's important that you take them in like fresh air so that they become your new reality. Remember, your brain cannot distinguish whether or not what you're seeing is real. When you feel wealthy, successful, secure or joyful, then it is real indeed. It's already happening and you'll attract more of it as same attracts the same. You'll become a magnet.

This will also change your beliefs and give you more trust, especially in yourself. Your doubts are based on bad experiences, so when you want to change your beliefs, you need to change your experiences. The good ones will lead to new ways of thinking.

And last but not least, once you have achieved one goal, such as your dream house, then acknowledge your inner power and replace that image with a new goal. You create what you think and feel; limitations only exist in your mind. You can decide how much you want and deserve. It's all up to you!

15

USING AFFIRMATIONS AND HYPNOSIS AS YOUR POWER SOURCES

WE TOUCHED UPON THE USE OF AFFIRMATIONS in a previous chapter, but I'd like to delve more deeply into this practice because I feel it's an extremely powerful tool in realizing our goals. As we previously discussed, affirmations are positive statements about any number of things in our lives. Indeed, the use of affirmations is a very old, proven technique and is still employed by many practitioners and doctors. What's magical about them is that when we use these affirmations to reinforce a positive attitude, we can achieve absolutely anything in our life.

So, how can affirmations help us? Remember when we spoke about those ongoing conversations we all have with ourselves? We discussed how we possess many different voices who talk to us pretty much at the same time, especially when an important decision is required of us. Think of it as having a meeting with different minded people who are all discussing what they're facing the at moment. These discussions, such as "Should I open my own business?" and the different opinions in our head are actually helping us to make the best possible decisions for ourselves because they allow us to view life and situations from different angles. In fact, we all have around 80,000 thoughts (voices) that are running through our heads every single day.

In that same chapter, I gave some examples of what these voices might be saying, but let's review some more examples for clarity. One voice, or let's say emotional state, might be frightened and in an inner conversation is telling us, "I haven't done something like that before. Maybe I should stay away because it's too big for me." At the same time, there's another voice who is more adventurous and loves to explore new things. This voice is probably telling us, "I'm so excited! I just can't wait to try this." Then there's the analytical voice who chimes in, "Let's first check the facts before we make a single move." Simultaneously, a restless voice – the one who doesn't have any patience – screams out, "Can we start now?" With all this chatter going on, the workaholic voice complains, "How can I manage this, too? I already have too much on my plate as it is!"

I know, all these voices in our head have us twisting and turning at times and it might seem difficult for us to find the right decision. Trust me, this is a good thing because we're viewing what's in front of us from different perspectives and approaches. It keeps our mind open until we finally discover the very best decision for ourselves. However, this is assuming that we've done some introspective work and are in touch with our inner emotions. We must be aware that these voices are coming from our subconsciousness and are based on past experiences. So, the question is, are we really in-touch and open-minded or are we static in our way of thinking – only with our brain? Are we open to new ways of reasoning or are we stuck in an ongoing, fearful "self-talk" and negative emotional state-of-being? Are these voices only helping us to find excuses why it's better to stay in our Comfort Zone and not try new things? If that's the case, then we're living our life on autopilot, without openly questioning things anymore.

Many of us are stuck in a pattern of always doing things the same way, keeping to a routine and sticking to old beliefs and behavior patterns. Even in our expectations, we are unable to deal with life and the world in an open-minded way. I call it a "Fear of Life." We just follow and do things as if they were fixed and programmed into our lives permanently. We exist and don't live to experience life anymore. That's when we become disconnected from ourselves and our souls. We lose creativity, spontaneity, excitement, joy and energy. Then we feel lifeless, depressed and lonely, easily caving in and not able to face the world with an open mindset. We think we already know what's going to happen and don't allow ourselves to create new life experiences. We simply mutate into living like robots.

There is a solution, though. These old, fixed thinking patterns that are rooted in past experiences can be transformed and programmed into different, positive and effective ways of creating new and better experiences by the use affirmations on a daily basis. It's a simple but extremely effective tool that we can count on every time. First, we should ask ourselves, "What do I think? What do I expect? Are my beliefs actualized and in healthy relation to reality or are they coming from past experiences and based on unrealistic prognoses?" As soon as we are aware of our thought patterns and inner voices, we are able to keep the ones that work for us and replace the ones which holds us back – those based on old, not updated beliefs. Let's take a look at how affirmations can help.

* * *

The use of affirmations is very similar to repeating Mantras. When repeated often, they create new ways of thinking and new beliefs that become deeply imbedded in our subconscious and our brains. We then begin to think, decide and act on a new level – one that we have chosen for ourselves. This new level encompasses the way we want to see and experience the world. We delete old and incorrect thoughts to make room for new, positive, optimistic and supportive beliefs and thought patters. We learn to face life with an open-minded attitude and that's when our inner conversations work for us and don't block us any longer.

So, what do affirmations look like? Well, they can be in the form of short, positive statements which reflect what we want and that in which we believe. A good place to start is to make a list of the different areas in our life and set particular intentions for ourselves. For example, do we always believe that we'll catch the flu every year? Who says so? Is it really true? If not, then create a new belief by writing down sentences such as:

I am strong.
I am healthy.
I will stay healthy and fit all season long.

It's best to use sentences that give us the feeling and impression that our immune system is so strong that we can survive any weather change or viruses during flu season. Of course, this includes taking care of ourselves, so when our intuition tells us to take a heavier jacket or wash our hands thoroughly, we should do it!

How do we traditionally think about money? Did our belief system always tell us, "Only selfish people earn a lot of money? It destroys people's characters and I wasn't meant for financial success in this life, anyway"? Well, we should turn that around, delete those sentences in our head and replace them with affirmations such as:

Money is an energy form.
I can do lots of good things with money.
Money comes easily to me.
Money is a source.
Money gives me security.
I love money.

We can do the same with our job or business by writing affirmations such as:

I am good at what I do.
I am outstanding.
I am a valuable person in this industry.
I can make it.
I can achieve whatever I want.
I have the power.
I can do it now.

What about our relationships? How about:

I am loveable.

I deserve to be loved.
I love.
I am kind.
I attract good people into my life.

It's easy to do, but the effectiveness of affirmations is formidable. We should therefore write down the most powerful sentences for each area of life and repeat them many times throughout our day. When we get up, while we're getting ready for work, when we're waiting on line, when we're on a train or in our car – everywhere! We should allow our affirmations to flow through our mind like mantras. We can also create one strong, single sentence which we repeat in our mind all day, like:

"I am healthy, strong, lovable, rich and happy."

It's important to be creative and find what works best for each one of us. When we do this and keep it up for a minimum of 4 weeks, we'll observe a change in our way of thinking.

Now, when we need to face challenges, we'll welcome them as old friends. We'll just stay in the vibration of our mantra and affirmations. We'll face these challenges with an open mind and react totally differently, saying "I am ready for this problem and will find a solution." Our way of viewing the difficulty will immediately change. We'll be more open, confident and capable of turning challenges into opportunities, becoming the master of our life. Our body will follow our mind and there will be a positive shift in our vital functions and lift in our constitution. When we use our mind as our power tool, we'll create everything from there.

Something to think about...

You can deepen the power of affirmations by the use of hypnosis. The period of time that lies just before you start to sleep and actually doze off is powerful in that your subconscious will take affirmations and sentences and deeply program them into your consciousness. How can you do that if your falling asleep? My best experience has been to download a version of a hypnosis audio book. There are lots of good ones available so you can actually choose one that speaks to your particular needs. There are books that focus on helping you to stop smoking, become free of anxiety, gain self-confidence, lose weight, stop procrastinating, and so on. The key and fundamental philosophy is that everything is energy and you can literally move situations, events and the material world by using your thoughts, energy, mind power and subconscious mindset to create what you would like to manifest. Just remember that it's important to listen to the hypnosis audio book every single evening for a minimum of 4 weeks.

So, how can you get started? It's easy...

- Choose an audio book with the content that speaks to what you want to shift or achieve in your life.
- Download it so it's easy to retrieve.
- Listen to it every evening when you go to bed and start to fall asleep.
- If you are not sleeping alone and don't want to disturb your partner, use earphones.

The great thing is, it doesn't matter if you actually fall asleep. Your brain will still receive the positive affirmations. Most of these books use a soft voice which repeats positive sentences and statements that speak to your desired goals. For example:

> All that you could do, you have done today.
> Now relax your body.
> Let go and enjoy the rest.
> Even if you start to sleep, you will hear my sentences.
> Your inner flame will always burn.
> You have the power within yourself.
> You are ready to live your dreams.
> You will know what to do.
> New opportunities will come into your life.
> Money is an energy and you will always have enough.
> It comes to you easily.
> Doors are going to open for you.
> You are successful.
> You are lovable.
> Life is exciting.
> You are strong.
> The universe has your back.

Now I will count to 10 and you are ready to start a new life.

1. You let go now of all negative things and thoughts.
2. You commit to yourself and your strength.
3. You start thinking positive.
4. You open up to new opportunities.

5. You believe in yourself.
6. You change what you want to change.
7. You trust in yourself.
8. You embrace the feeling of having it already.
9. You are grateful for all that you have.
10. You start to live your dreams.

Of course, repeating affirmations to yourself, while you're awake, is a powerful tool in and of itself. Listening to hypnosis during that "twilight" time, just before you sleep or even when you are already sleeping, just acts as a reprogramming mechanism. That's how hypnosis works. It gives you a new way of seeing and believing things by implanting them in your brain. After just a few days, your thoughts will automatically move in a new, positive direction and your body, in turn, will follow. This, of course, will impact your behavior and habits. Your attitude and self-belief will change and you'll start acting in a more positive way.

If you really have the desire to change and shift your life, your beliefs and your emotions, you now have another very powerful tool at hand. Get motivated, discipline yourself and let affirmations and hypnosis become part of your daily routine and lifestyle. In the long-term, it will change your life the way you want.

HOW TO USE YOUR INTUITION

"INTUITION" OR "GUT FEELING" ARE OFTEN-USED WORDS but how do we know for sure that it's really our intuition and not just a feeling or thought that pops into our mind? That's a good question, so let's examine what exactly intuition is and how to recognize it.

I like to think of my intuition as the "Other Side of Me," – the part that is connected to the unknown, the place from where we all originated. To develop a strong awareness of our intuition – this other side of us – it's important to first build a relationship with it. The fact that our intuition is indeed a part of us explains why it helps us to discover all the answers in our own body and heart. But we need to stop thinking and analyzing, which I'll explain more. For the moment, though, it's crucial to understand that we must not visualize our intuition as something apart and separate from whom we are. It only makes sense, then, that in order to be able to count on our intuition and not get irritated over mixed messages and feelings, it's important to first have a loving relationship with ourselves – the source of our intuition. Self-love and self-care are the beginning of a deep connection to our intuition. When we stop judging ourselves and instead give ourselves permission to think and feel good about us – exactly as we are and feel – and trust ourselves, fully, then we'll create space for deeper answers and intuitive guidance to appear.

It's important to remember that to use our intuition to find all of the answers for which we're searching in our body, we need to be silent at times. We need to breathe and arrive at that place from whence we came. We are consciousness and all connected. We can feel the right answers from us when we search inside ourselves. All we need to do is to trust and act as soon as we have found the answer. No matter what it looks like. Let's explore that more.

* * *

There exists analytical brain movement which is involved in being intuitive and guided by our intuition. Let me give you an example. When Evelyn looks for a good doctor by searching online and visiting different websites, she will experience "first impressions." Perhaps she'll come across a website that appeals to her in that she likes the colors of the page and the photo of the doctor gives her the feeling that he or she is competent. She's also impressed by the doctor's bio. The only problem is that the practice is far from Evelyn's home or office. So, she keeps searching other websites. She runs across one that doesn't appeal to her the way the first did, but the office is close by. So, she keeps reading about the doctor's practice. Evelyn is still not getting that trustworthy and welcoming feeling the first website gave her, but this doctor seems professional enough and the office is conveniently close. So, she books an appointment.

Perhaps on the day of Evelyn's visit to the doctor's office, everything goes wrong. She wakes up late because she set "pm" instead of "am" on her alarm clock. There's traffic on the road because it's raining cats and dogs. She also forgot her umbrella! It seems like everything is trying to keep her from getting to that appointment. Do you think Evelyn made the right decision about this doctor?

Here's the thing. Intuition is like a feather. It's silent and almost not visible or recognizable. It's the VERY FIRST "impulse" before our brain starts analyzing. We therefore need to tune into a state of awakening meditation, where we just observe. We have to trust our intuition – that first silent impulse – and take action without questioning it. I'm fairly certain – given my experiences with my own intuition – that Evelyn probably did not make the right decision here. If she had a great feeling about the first doctor's website – even though his or her office is further away and not so convenient – chances are this doctor is the one for her at the moment. By choosing the second doctor, Evelyn is energetically blocked because she didn't get that everything happens for a reason, even if she doesn't understand it. Her soul understands it, though. She just didn't allow things to flow the way they were supposed to, and that's not a good way to start a relationship with a doctor, or anyone.

* * *

IN THE STORM OF LIFE

We've all made mistakes by not listening to our intuition! I don't worry about what's in the past. At the end of the day, time and space are an illusion. It's all about the experience. We just need to remember that our intuition knows the bigger picture of our life. We have to start listening to our intuition more and act (within reason) on it before our brain goes into its analytical mode. Perhaps, in taking immediate action upon that intuition, something we never imagined is waiting for us. Maybe we'll unexpectedly meet a person who will become very important to us. Or we might come across a property for lease – just like the one for which we've been searching. We might even pass a pet shop and fall in love with a puppy in the window, the one we bring home and changes our life in an unbelievably positive way! Our intuition is our compass in the darkness. It has more wisdom and knowledge than you or I could ever have. It's connected to our very soul, the plan of the journey we've chosen, and the universal mind. It is pure consciousness and connected to the pure potential of life.

* * *

It's quite comforting and even empowering to recognize intuition as our guardian, our medium, our wise companion. The closer and more connected we become with it, the more confident we'll feel when we receive its messages. Remember, our intuition talks to us when we're in a "non-thinking" state-of-mind. It's always the very first impulse, trigger and touch before our mind starts to think and scrutinize. To illustrate this further, let's say, for example, Joseph is apartment hunting and the moment he steps into a potential building he smells something bad. He gets the immediate impression that he should be careful, that there's something strange here and he shouldn't trust it. He should stop there! Joseph shouldn't let his mind start making excuses for the bad smell, telling him that it has no bearing on whether or not he should take an apartment there. On the opposite side of the coin, Danielle's realtor sends her to an apartment that's in a part of town in which she didn't see herself living. Something tells her to go and see it anyway, and the moment she enters it she already feels a bit of excitement. Something is pulling her in a magical way and she's feeling like a child who's discovering something with an open, innocent and excited mind. That's her intuition trying to tell her, "Take it! Where your heart beats higher is the way."

So, we should always be on the lookout for our intuition. Whenever we have certain feelings or impressions before we even start to think about something, that's our intuition communicating with us. Again, remember that a deep relationship with our intuition is necessary to be able to trust in a way that allows us to take action. We often won't see or understand what would happen if we didn't take its advice, or why we should take it at all. That's not necessary for us to know. All we need to do is trust that what isn't meant for us shouldn't be in our life anyway. We must let it go. Maybe at some stage we'll understand why. Our intuition always has our back.

* * *

When it comes to people – both in our personal and business life – our intuition is our best compass to understanding them properly and realizing the impact they will have on us. Just as we said in the beginning of this chapter, our first impression is very important, so we need to trust it. However, we must also keep in mind that people often come across differently when we first meet them and, after a while, they grow on us as we begin to understand and like them. In the case of inter-social contact and communications, I think it's best to observe how we FEEL right before and after meeting someone. How did we FEEL during our time with them? Did we want to get out of the room or stay? Were we tired and drained? Irritated or uplifted and excited? Did we kind of miss the person after meeting him or her, even looking forward to our next meeting? Or perhaps we felt that we weren't so keen on meeting them again, at least not in the near future?

In terms of people, our intuition talks to us very loudly, throughout our entire body. In addition, we'll find the answers when we're alone again. Whatever our unanalyzed impression is serves as a great guide on to how to deal with that person. We should observe our body before, during and after contact and then we'll find the answers for which we're looking. If we really like a person and enjoy spending time with him or her, we don't have to think or say it aloud. We'll FEEL vibrant, energetic, cheerful and happy and that's exactly what that person will pick up. If we're down, tired and just looking to leave, the person will pick that up too and it will push them away. So, in many cases, our intuition and how our body reacts to it will also help the other person to know whether or not the relationship will work as well. And even if that person is only living in his or her head and ignores these signs, wanting to keep going with a connection that doesn't nourish us, we can set healthy boundaries. Yes, when dealing with people, it's very difficult to rely on a poker face. We're all so connected to similar energies. We all vibrate and pick up each other's energy, whether we want to or not. We should use this to our advantage. We must not concentrate on what people say to us. The truth about what they really mean to us and how they think about us will show up as signals in our body.

* * *

The more we start trusting our intuition, the more we'll be in balance with ourselves and the world because it will guide us through our personal, best version of our journey. It's a spiritual awakening as we connect to much deeper levels of ourselves and the universe. We'll be able to use energy and vibrations to our advantage. We'll change our focus from the outside world to the inside of ourselves. We'll become the observer of the bigger picture of ourselves and the world by seeing and realizing the energetic truth that lies in between words and actions. All at the same time, we'll be active. We'll become more and more enthusiastically meditative and that will offer us the possibility of using the universal laws and energies for our personal journey. It's all waiting for us, so we should take advantage of the gifts our intuition gives us and soar freely and happily!

Something to think about...

Learning to use our intuition takes time and practice. If you're struggling in the beginning, that's perfectly normal. Just write down how you felt during various activities during your day. The goal is to shift yourself from a state of permanently thinking and analyzing to always feeling first.

Ask yourself...

- What am I feeling?
- Where in my body do I feel it?
- How exactly does that feel?

Recognition is the key. Instead of immediately reacting, just observe what is really going on inside of you. Become an observer of yourself. Your body is like a letter box that contains messages from your intuition.

- Quiet your mind.
- Don't think.
- Just feel.
- Breathe and see what comes up.

Deep breathing brings you into a state of NO THINKING. There you will receive the messages from your intuition and the universal mind. You'll find your answers.

- Then act!
- Act without questioning your answers.

Often you won't understand why you're feeling that something is right or wrong.

- Don't try to understand it.

- Just act on it.
- You don't need to know why.

Yes, trusting your intuition totally will come to you easier with time. Of course, the stronger and deeper your relationship is with your intuition, the more effortless it will become.

Always remember that intuition is part of recognition and self-love. When you observe how you feel in terms of what happens, you'll recognize yourself in that situation. When you love yourself, you will accept your feelings and can trust and follow your intuition and no one and nothing can make you feel badly about that. Connecting and following your intuition will bring you back home – to yourself, to your soul and to the very personal journey you have chosen for this life. Always remember, where your heart beats higher is your way!

THE POWER OF GRATITUDE: IT'S ALL ABOUT VIBRATION

WHEN I FIRST HEARD ABOUT THE POWER of gratitude some years ago, I was in a different frame of mind than now. I thought, "How can I be grateful if I have to live a challenging life where I'm always feeling lost and just too busy surviving? Where existential fears are my daily companions?" Then I sat back and thought about it. Even if I wasn't really feeling it or even able to fully understand the message and the whole impact of being grateful, I had nothing to lose anyway. So, I started practicing gratitude. Every morning I woke up and focused on what I love and how grateful I was for those things and slowly but surely things started to shift for me. When I walked through the day, I would keep gratitude in mind. One day, for example, I received a complimentary gift from a cosmetic brand and instead of just saying thank you, I embraced the feeling that I was a magnet for abundance and was so grateful for it. In return, more and more wonderful things showed up in my life. I felt differently, and the more I focused on being grateful for different things the better life became for me. Of course, it took time, but at least challenges didn't feel quite as heavy anymore. I saw them in a different light.

The truth is, gratitude is a vibration. In fact, being grateful is like switching on the light. We cannot fight against the darkness, but when the light appears, darkness immediately vanishes. It's the same with gratitude. When we embrace it, depression and every feeling of lack disappears. Because one of the laws of the universe is that like things attracts like things, when we focus on what we're missing, we get more of nothing. However, when we focus with gratitude on what we already have – as well as embrace our feeling of being abundant as we already have so much in our life – then we attract more of that. And, no matter where we are in any moment of our life, there are always so many things for which we can truly be grateful.

Make no mistake about it: Nothing is as powerful as the vibration of being grateful. It's an immediate shift from lacking to having, from poorness to abundance, from isolation to being loved. It puts us in a state of being positive, of having faith, of living in our power and of having a foundation of feeling supported instead of being a victim who's lost, powerless, helpless and depressed. We must remember, though, that the most important thing about embracing gratitude is that it must come a sense of being abundant, rather than being grateful that we are just surviving. That is the hidden secret behind gratitude. People often tell me, "I am so happy to have a roof over my head and a job." But that feeling of gratitude is based on fear and will not change our lives in a way that attracts more positive things. The feeling of gratitude I am talking about, which can truly change our entire life and brings with it a much higher level of living, is the feeling of being abundant. Being a king or a queen, being strong, loved, powerful and truly grateful for being such a rich person. Waking up and feeling this gift of being alive, healthy, strong, loved and surrounded of abundance. That feeling will attract more of the same.

I also find that feeling grateful is like being in love – with ourselves and with the world. It brings us to a much higher frequency and disconnects us from fears, anxiety, anger, depression and frustration. When we begin to practice gratitude, we might at first feel like we're faking it as we struggle with certain issues, not feeling particularly blessed at the moment. However, when we're really committed to changing our circumstances and ready to make a big shift toward being successful, happy and in control of our life, things start to change. We suddenly make the right decisions and take reasonable actions. We are motivated to start with setting some intentions, taking steps and beginning to express our grateful feelings on a daily basis. You see, it's our perspective of things that makes the difference. When we shift that to one of gratitude, then in return what we think is what we attract.

* * *

Gratitude is like love, another one of the highest vibrations in the universe. As such, it has an immediate impact on our emotions, mental mood and health. Remember that everything we do is either because we're afraid of something or because we love doing it. We always act out of fear or love. We can use gratitude like medicine. This deep feeling of being grateful for our life and certain things influences our wellbeing, physical body, emotional state of being and mental health. The vibration of gratitude is like that of sound. Any vibration affects our body on such a deep level that it's seen in the physical form. As we've discussed in a previous chapter, our bodies are comprised of 80% water and as such vibrations affect the composition of our molecules. Harmonious music, for example, lifts our bodies and emotions and aggressive music lowers them. Since gratitude is all about vibrations, and as we are magnets where same attracts the same, we have with being grateful a powerful tool at hand – one that can alter and control our wellbeing entirely. We can immediately change and become a strong magnet for abundance, joy, love and health.

* * *

It is proven that practicing gratitude makes us happy. Indeed, it's a happiness source. The Harvard Health Publishing medical School shared in an article: "The word gratitude is derived from the Latin word *gratia*, which means grace, graciousness, or gratefulness (depending on the context). In some ways gratitude encompasses all of these meanings." Gratitude therefore can become much more interesting and inspiring when we think of its meaning in relation to grace. That's even more reason to start embracing our attitude and focus on gratitude. Whenever life is challenging, we need to focus back on that for which we are grateful. Very often, there is something in the difficult situation that will ultimately connect with something for which we can be grateful, and that lifts our feelings and vibration. Only when we vibrate on a higher frequency do we attract the positive side of life. It's so important to remember that the feelings we experience around gratitude are the key to changing and improving our lives.

We should therefore all put on our keychain or carry in our pockets something that reminds us of all the things for which we can be grateful. In the book "The Secret," Rhonda Byrne talks about a gratitude stone or rock. This reminder of always being in the vibration of gratitude has healed people from illnesses and influence positive outcomes for many different situations and events.

Gratitude will change our life on a deep level and allow us to concentrate on the good things and on what we like, expect and want more abundantly. This is so much more desirable than being stuck in a mode of complaining about what's not working. It keeps us in a thought pattern of positive expectations, which will in turn influence outcomes in a positive way.

* * *

I have lived in some different and very exotic countries and have seen people in all types of circumstances. Even now, while I live in South Africa which I love very much, things like electricity are not guaranteed. I often see people living in terrible conditions – hungry, broken, without shoes and homeless. This really affects my attitude and makes me so incredibly grateful for my life and all that I have, including my talents and blessings, friends, family and health.

Then when I travel back to Europe, I realize how rich these countries truly are. I enjoy coming home to where I was born and am so grateful for being able to take a shower without rushing so that the water doesn't run out. Abundant water and electricity are something you can always count on there. It's all about perspective and how we see the world. The way in which we see things is the way in which they show up in our lives.

Traveling so much, I often observe how much people complain when their flights are delayed. They get so frustrated and it sometimes baffles me. Are these delays really such a big deal in the scope of their whole lives? Of course not. We can keep complaining about things which don't work or start embracing the grace, fascination and gratitude about all of the amazing things in our life. That's always our choice. Life is magical and only our ego can separate us from this preferable perspective. Fighting, suffering and frustration will always arise when we are attached to what our analytical minds *believe* is reality or how it should be. However, only when we change the focus from our ego to our heart and embrace the true magic of our true self – which we cannot see or describe but is still there – will our life transform. These types of problems, such as delayed flights or trains, etc. will become silly to us. Then we'll start solving our problems by being flexible and making it work instead of losing energy by complaining. In addition, we'll start swimming with the flow of life instead of against it.

We all should see our life through grateful eyes, hugging and loving it all. Our life will be so valuable, joyful and amazing in ways that we could never have thought possible.

All of our power is inside ourselves – our thoughts and our feelings. Gratitude is our secret key to having it all. It brings us to the stars and will totally transform us like a cocoon to a butterfly, allowing us to step into our true energy – being love, being part of all that exists, being a creator.

Some things to think about...

Here are some powerful tools and examples that you can use to immediately start your journey to being grateful. They will help you improve your awareness of this powerful energy, embrace self-love and welcome positive shifts in your life.

- When you wake up in the morning, be grateful for the new day and what you have. Feel this emotion and embrace it. Think of your family, your loved ones, your pet, your health, your home, your job – all that you have learned and experienced so far and for this brand-new day.

- Write a gratitude journal. Every evening, when you are back from work or before you start to sleep, think about 3 things from that day for which you are grateful. In the morning, set an intention for one thing for which you want to be grateful. How will you show your grateful vibration? What do you want to achieve so that when evening comes, you can proclaim your gratitude for it? Observe your feelings and mood during the day. Did you feel a change, a shift?

IN THE STORM OF LIFE

- Start focusing on all the small things in your life, the ones for which you are already grateful. Perhaps it's your bed, having electricity, enough water to shower, a delicious cup of coffee, a smile from someone, a simple gift, or even an unexpected discount! This will make you so much more present and bring you into the moment – right now, where all your life is happening.

www.ingramcontent.com/pod-product-compliance
Lightning Source LLC
Chambersburg PA
CBHW070442090426
42735CB00012B/2437